Lost Houses of County D

PETER MEADOWS & EDWARD WATE

Foreword by Lucinda Lambton

Ravensworth Castle

JILL RAINES
1993

FOREWORD

Despite nestling under the wing of Durham Cathedral, one of the greatest buildings on this earth, the county of Durham is sadly no longer famed for its great houses. This was not always the case. Before the gobbling tide of coal mining and industrialisation had eaten up so much of the countryside, Durham was thick with distinguished houses, both great and small, that would match up to any of the swank and stately trails today, and this book has triumphed in showing us the splendours that once were. With a wealth of scholarly and sympathetic detail, it plunges you back into this forgotten past of the county.

What a joy, for example, to discover that Elizabeth Barrett Browning was born in the Gothick Coxhoe Hall and that 'Bonnie Bobby Shafto' lived at Whitworth Hall, near Spennymoor in the late 1700s. It is pure pleasure too, to read that at c.18th Hylton Castle (now a shell, surrounded by a housing estate) there were stuccoed ceilings with Venus and Cupid and with 'Apollo fiddling to the Gods, Minerva in her helmet and an old King'.

What tantalising tears we shed as we read page after painful page of this book, with each one giving us yet another glimpse of a beautiful building that is no more. We should make amends, however feebly, for our past folly in allowing so many of these houses to disappear, and, armed with this book as our bible, we should set off to honour these sad shells of architectural masterpieces. In many, in fact most cases, the buildings have gone altogether, but thanks to our guide *Lost Houses of Durham* we can sleuth-like seek out traces of their existence, or at least pay homage to the site on which they stood. What about a journey to Glamis Castle to see the great fireplace of Hercules and Samson that was rescued from Gibside near Gateshead when it was gutted in 1920? And how I would enjoy searching for evidence of the 18th century Gateshead Park House in the industrial building that rose up around its remains. There is ceaseless delight to be gained from such seemingly secret knowledge. What good fun to know that the Visitors Centre at Beamish Hall Open Air Museum was once the c.18th stables of Greencroft Hall near Lanchester. With this book at hand you will be able, as if by magic, to peer into the past. How pleasant, for example, to stand in the middle of the Team Valley Trading Estate, knowing that you are on the site of Farnacres 'a long house with a sweeping verandah' complete with a private museum and lived in by F. W. Bernard, 'The Low Fell Giant' or to track down the site of Stella Hall in Blaydon where you will be knocked out by nostalgia. In the middle of the modern housing there once stood a great 17th century pile that was aggrandised in the 1700s by James Paine. Swags of ornate plasterwork swooped through all the rooms, most particularly in the drawing room where they were embellished by plaster palm trees, a framed landscape in plaster and a shooting star in honour of the house. In the 1850s both Garibaldi and Orsini were entertained amid these classical splendours; a hundred years later, in the 1950s, Stella Hall was demolished for a housing estate. Having all this information at your finger tips is a poignant blessing.

Consett rolled over 17th century Crook Hall; Gateshead crushed Deckham's Hall of 1614 and an 'executive home' replaced the Victorian Broadwood Hall, at Lanchester, in the 1960s. Most evocative of all is the glimpse given to us of Coxhoe Hall; we are told that as well as having sumptuously swirling plasterwork inside, the gardens too were magnificent, laid out at bankrupting expense. The hill on which Coxhoe was built was alive with 'innumerable tame rabbits of many colours and varieties', of which sadly no traces remain. This book is stuffed with such sorry tales, but even sorrier would have been not to relate them. By hauling them all from the past the *Lost Houses of Durham* have been given a new and glowing presence in the county.

Lucinda Lambton

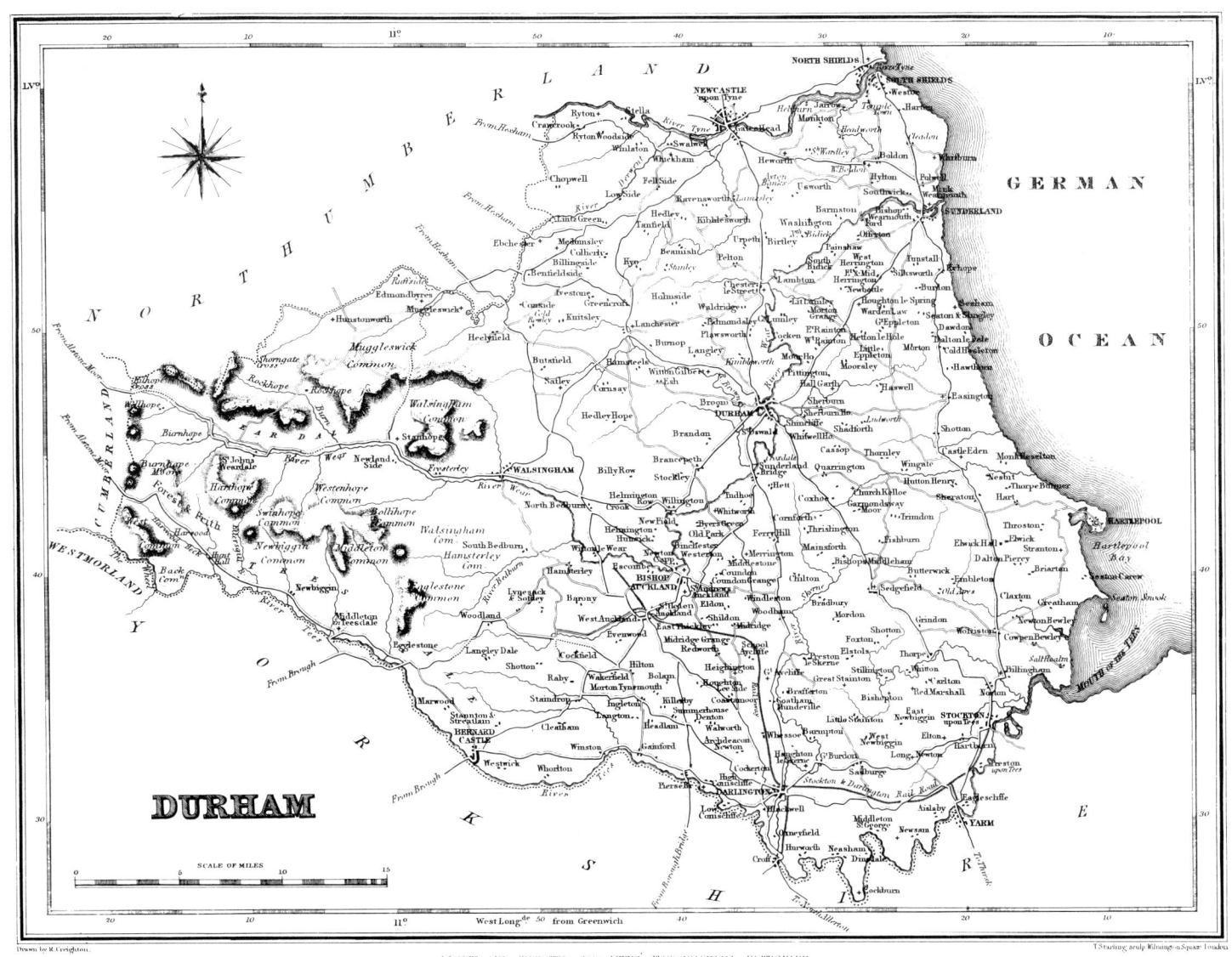

County Durham c.1835 (O'Flynn Books)

INTRODUCTION

County Durham, the land between the Tees and the Tyne, conjures up two powerful images: the Palatinate, where the Prince-Bishop held temporal and spiritual sway, with his stronghold at Durham Castle, his palace at Auckland, and his imposing cathedral in Durham; and coal-mines, pit-wheels, spoil-heaps and villages of straggling terraces. But the palatinate has gone, abolished in 1836, and its Bishop is merely a diocesan; and now the last coal mine in the county has closed. Beyond the conurbations of South Tyneside, Wearside and Teesside, County Durham is becoming rural once again.

The county's landscape provides sharp contrasts. Rolling countryside gives way to sudden, hidden valleys, such as Durham itself, low when seen from afar, but towering on its peninsula when seen close-up. The starkest contrast has been between the rural and the industrial. Coal dominated parts of the county for several centuries: it was mined in the Tyne and Wear valleys from the 17th century. In the 18th century it spread south, and in the 19th century there was an explosion of activity, spurred on by technological innovations which made deep-mined coal a realistic proposition. Over about two-thirds of County Durham mines operated. Other industries sprang up also — steelmaking in the Derwent valley in the 17th century, chemical works on Tyneside, and later in North Teesside, shipbuilding at Sunderland and West Hartlepool, ironworks at Consett, round Bishop Auckland, and Teesside.

It would be wrong, however, to suppose that the county was wholly devoted to industry. There was the usual pattern of rural estates, supported by agricultural revenues. Yet what was perhaps remarkable about County Durham was the willingness of landowners to tolerate, encourage and actively invest in industry, especially coal-mines. In the 18th century the 'Grand Alliance' of landowners in the north of the county sought to control the coal-trade with London. In the 19th century this participation became almost frenetic. Every landowner wished to exploit the coal resources under his estate. With the royalties, huge seats could be built and maintained, such as Ravensworth Castle, Lambton Castle and Wynyard Park. Opulence founded on coal could sometimes be literally undermined by it: Lambton Castle had to be expensively underpinned when old workings gave way beneath it in the 1850s, and houses such as Ravensworth Castle and Coxhoe Hall had to be abandoned and demolished in the mid-20th century after subsidence. Other houses were eventually too close to the mines, works and factories to be attractive places in which to live: the families moved to other seats, and the houses became the manager's house, or the offices, or even (in the case of Park House, Gateshead) industrial buildings. Such was the fate of Crook Hall near Consett, Hylton Castle, Sunderland, and Birtley Hall.

County Durham has had a string of notable historians, including William Hutchinson (1783-94), Robert Surtees (1816-40), and Mackenzie and Ross (1834); but the sources of old illustrations are poor. Topographical artists were attracted by the great antiquities of the county, the cathedral, the castles, and the monastic remains. There is no Samuel Buck sketchbook for Durham to compare with the Yorkshire volume of houses of c.1718 (though Samuel and Nathaniel Buck did publish several engravings in 1728, including the lost houses of Hylton Castle and Ravensworth). Knyff and Kip did not illustrate any Durham houses in *Britannia illustrata* (1707); but an unknown mid-18th century topographer made a bird's eye view of Cocken Hall and its estate which is the best illustration of that interesting house.

Many Durham houses were obscure and were demolished or abandoned before the mid-19th century invention of photography. Indeed, many houses were called 'hall' which were really no more than farmhouses. Houghall Hall, Durham, which had some interesting 17th century features, is illustrated in this book; most others are not. Sometimes the only illustration of a house is a gloomy photograph of a derelict building with pit-heaps or chimneys looming close, the house boarded up and awaiting demolition. It is fortunate that *Country Life* recorded the interiors of Streatlam Castle near Barnard Castle before that house was sold by the Bowes-Lyon family, Earls of Strathmore, in 1927. An unknown photographer recorded the splendours of Ravensworth Castle's interiors before it became a school in the 1930's, and there are good series of interior photographs of Stella Hall, near Gateshead, and Neasham Hall, near Darlington, and glimpses of the rococo interiors of Coxhoe Hall.

The architects of some notable lost houses are not known. Streatlam Castle, Greencroft Hall, Helmington Hall, Crook Hall, Newton Hall and Usworth House were late 17th or early 18th century houses whose designers are unrecorded. It would be interesting to know more about the designers of Robert Wharton's Old Park, an important Gothick house of the 1760's, in which the poet Thomas Gray is thought to have had a hand; and whether Charles Lyon's new-built Binchester Hall, bought by the Bishop in 1832 and soon demolished, and nearby Newton Cap Hall, started in the 1760's but never completed, were distinguished buildings. Several eminent architects did work in County Durham, including James Gibbs at Gateshead Park, James Paine at Ravensworth Castle, Daniel Garrett at Gibside and (probably) Hylton Castle. John Nash at Ravensworth, Joseph Bonomi and his son Ignatius at Lambton Castle, Phillip Wyatt at Red Hall, Haughton-le-Skerne, and John Dobson at Cleadon Cottage, Birtley Hall, Lambton Castle, Hawthorn Tower and Neasham Hall.

In the 19th century suburban seats, miniature estates of successful industrialists and businessmen, were established around Gateshead, South Shields, Sunderland, West Hartlepool, Stockton and Darlington. Some were modest villas, while others were major mansions. As the towns expanded, most of them ceased to be residences: the park was sold for housing, the house might become an institution, or else be demolished. A selection of the most interesting or important 19th century houses has been made; many others have had to be excluded.

Much still remains in County Durham, though perhaps fewer houses have survived in family hands than in other counties of England. Lord Barnard owns Raby Castle; Brancepeth Castle, long a regimental museum, has been reclaimed as a residence; the Salvins are at Croxdale Hall, and the Lambtons at Biddick Hall. Elemore Hall, with fine 18th century plasterwork, and Windlestone Hall, the former seat of the Edens, are county schools, and Burn Hall, Ignatius Bonomi's bold neoclassical house for Bryan Salvin, is a retreat centre. Lumley Castle is in institutional use; Wynyard Park, formerly the seat of the Marquess of Londonderry, has been bought by Sir John Hall. Several houses have become country house hotels.

The principles of inclusion of houses are as in previous volumes in this series. Mediæval castles and houses ruined for centuries have been excluded. Houses demolished before 1900 and not rebuilt on the same site are described, as are houses lost since 1900, even where a new house was built on the site. A few houses of exceptional interest, which survive as gutted shells, such as Gibside and Hylton Caastle, or which have been substantially reduced, such as Lambton Castle, or whose future is very uncertain, such as Saltwell Towers, have been included.

The descriptions are mostly too brief to be full histories of the houses illustrated. In many instances it has been extremely difficult to discover the 20th century history of County Durham houses. Additional information about the houses in this book, and about significant lost houses not included, will be particularly welcome. The authors would be most interested to know of good illustrations, photographs and postcards of County Durham houses, and architectural drawings and sale catalogues, and would appreciate the loan of such material for copying.

STREATLAM CASTLE, Barnard Castle

The seat of the Bowes family, and later the Bowes-Lyon Earls of Strathmore, east of Barnard Castle in upper Teesdale, was gutted in 1927 and demolished with dynamite in a Territorial Army exercise in 1959.

It was an imposing early 18th century house, fronting an old building rebuilt by Sir William Bowes about 1450. Sir William was in France in the 15th century with the Duke of Bedford, and according to Hutchinson he sent home "a model and plan of his castle of Streatlam... [and] rebuilt the Castle after a Norman model."

The new castle was probably begun by Sir William Bowes (1656-1706). Extensive quarrying operations are recorded for 1717-18, and the house was called "very near finished" in 1720. It was a suite of rooms one-room deep with a passage and staircase behind. The thirteen bay front had projecting wings, and was three storeys high, in a plain classical style, with little wooden cupolas on the roof. The façade was enlivened with banded rustication, and the parapets had balustrades. Hutchinson criticised the siting of the house as "gloomy and confined" and added "nothing but a veneration for the ancient seat of the family, could induce Sir William Bowes to erect such a mansion, in so ineligible a situation... there is something romantic in such secluded scenes, but they are better suited to the vicinity of a cottage than a palace."

Two sons of Sir William died young, and George Bowes succeeded in 1721, holding the estates until 1761. He preferred

(1) Streatlam Castle, front (Darlington Centre for Local Studies)
(2) Streatlam Castle ruins, 1959 (The Northern Echo)

to live at Gibside, and had a house at St. Paul's Walden, Hertfordshire. His only daughter Mary Eleanor (1749-1800) married the 9th Earl of Strathmore (d.1776). She then married an adventurer, Lieut. Andrew Robinson Stoney, who took the name Bowes, was elected M.P. for Newcastle, and entertained grandly at her houses. He ran through her money and treated her cruelly, so that she finally appealed to Chancery for protection. He kidnapped her and tried to make her sign away her property. She finally obtained a divorce, and he was committed to King's Bench Prison. She was succeeded by her son, the 10th Earl of Strathmore (1769-1820).

John Bowes (1811-85), founder of the Bowes Museum at Barnard Castle, was an illegitimate son of the 10th Earl (although his mother married the Earl the day before his death). He did not inherit the title, but received the County Durham estates, which included Gibside as well as Streatlam. He grew immensely rich on coal royalties. John and Benjamin Green of Newcastle, architects, were employed to make alterations in 1840-42. They added a portico and rebuilt the cupolas in stone. Later, in 1878, Bowes consulted Jules Pellechet, architect of Bowes Museum, and employed John Edward Watson to make internal alterations. The dining room was given a heavy armorial ceiling in oak, featuring the arms of Bowes' ancestors, the library had a panelled ceiling, and the drawing room ceiling was painted with sky and clouds. This ceiling seems to have disappeared when photographs of the rooms were

(3) Rear View (Darlington Centre for Local Studies)
(4) Drawing room (Country Life)

taken in 1915. In the grounds, a new orangery was built to receive orange trees brought from Louveciennes in 1862.

On Bowes' death in 1885 the castle and the Durham estates reverted to his cousin, the 13th Earl of Strathmore. *Country Life* illustrated Streatlam in 1915, when the rooms were still furnished. The estate was sold piecemeal by Lord Strathmore between 1922 and 1927. In 1927 the fittings were sold at auction. The armorial ceiling found its way eventually into the Bowes Museum, where it can still be seen.

Norman and Elsie Field of Lartington Hall, Yorkshire bought the estate and used the outbuildings as a stud. They removed the Castle's roof. The Army occupied the building in 1939-45. After the war the estate was sold to a member of the Pease family.

(5) *Boudoir (Country Life)*
(6) *Streatlam Castle, view from library (Country Life)*
(7) *Dining Room (Country Life)*

SNOTTERTON HALL, Staindrop

No illustration is known of Snotterton, demolished 1831 for a farmhouse, Raby Grange, now Snotterton Hall Farm. It was a late Gothic house, with three-light mullioned windows under square heads, an embattled parapet and corner pinnacles. The Bainbridge family owned Snotterton in the 16th century: their arms were carved over the entrance. In 1607 George Bainbridge sold Snotterton to Toby Ewbanke of Staindrop Hall. Later the Smart family of which Christopher Smart the poet was a member) were the owners, and c.1790 it was sold by Mr. Smart, a London solicitor, to the Earl of Darlington, of Raby Castle.

HOPPYLAND PARK, Bedburn

Hoppyland Park, in forty acres of grounds close to grouse moors, was gutted in 1952, and now stands ruined, half-demolished and engulfed with ivy.

It was an old house mostly destroyed by fire (maliciously, apparently) in 1793, and reconstructed with a mock castle front of turrets and battlements. There were four turrets of varying outline. This thin, amateur Gothick trim was effective when seen from a distance, but disappointing when examined closely. The windows were conventional sashes, and the detailing — the slits and cross-openings on the turrets — was rudimentary. Hoppyland had none of the ingenuity of Thomas Wharton's Gothick Old Park of thirty years earlier.

Few features of the older house, which was one room deep, survived, except for a crudely-detailed 17th century staircase, and one 16th and one late 17th century fireplace.

The estate was purchased in 1619 by Edward Blackett, and was sold in 1768 by John Blackett to George Leaton Blenkinsopp of Whickham, near Gateshead. Hoppyland remained in the Blenkinsopp family until the early 20th century: in 1857 Thomas Leaton Blenkinsopp was the owner, and in 1908 George Ilderton Leaton Blenkinsopp. It descended from the Blenkinsopps to Mrs. Izat, and c.1926 it was bought by Lieutenant-Colonel Thomas Dowling, a Bishop Auckland solicitor.

(1) Hoppyland Park (Beamish Museum)
(2) Rear view, ruins (RCHM England)

Samuel & Nathaniel Buck, view of Auckland Castle, 1728. Newton Cap is top left, Binchester Hall is top right.

NEWTON CAP HALL, Bishop Auckland

Newton Cap is shown in Buck's view of Auckland Castle. A new Hall, built in the mid-18th century, was unfinished, and by 1834 both Halls were ruinous.

John Bacon (1655-1736) bought the estate c.1699. His son William (d.1748) married Margaret Forster, and made alterations (a rainwater head with their arms was dated 1747). John Bacon Forster (d.1767) started the new Hall; his son William Bacon Forster continued it. William "led a profligate life, squandering his property in extravagance and gaming" (Whellan); Conyers Surtees says his wife Lady Catherine (d.1780) had "extravagant habits, embarrassing his affairs". Soon after remarrying, he committed suicide in the unfinished Hall. His posthumous son, William Forster, died in 1810 aged 30.

The sale notice (*Tyne Mercury*, 9 Jan. 1810) described shady banks, tall oaks in the park, a Hall lately built on a better site, and a 2-acre walled garden. William Russell of Brancepeth bought Newton Cap in 1812. It passed to his daughter, wife of Sir Gordon Drummond, and granddaughter, who married the Earl of Effingham in 1832. The two halls were unoccupied: Mackenzie & Ross (1834) called them "for some years... in a state of rapid decay".

Lord Effingham sold Newton Cap to Stobart & Co., Newton Cap Colliery. They demolished one Hall in 1870. The other passed to Bolckow and Vaughan, ironmasters, who demolished it in 1868.

BINCHESTER HALL

The Earl of Westmorland lost Binchester after the 1569 rebellion. Anthony Wren (d.1595) bought it. Binchester was early 17th century. Hutchinson called it "a fine old building... composed of a centre and two wings." One wing had a semi-circular bracketed window; the north wing was remodelled. Buck's view shows Binchester Hall opposite the Bishop's residence.

After the death of Farrer Wren (1715-94), Binchester passed to his daughter Mary (d.1814), who married (1744) Thomas Lyon, third son of the 8th Earl of Strathmore. Her second son Charles Lyon inherited Binchester. He rebuilt the Hall "upon a very beautiful plan". He invested heavily in coal mines and attempted a pit at Binchester, but water problems exhausted his resources. To avoid a mine so close to his palace the Bishop decided to buy Binchester. The Binchester Estates Act (1828) allowed him to sell Church land elsewhere. Binchester was advertised for sale in 1829.

After the sale Charles Lyon refused to leave, claiming unfair treatment. He finally left in May 1833. The empty Hall was demolished in March 1835. Matthew Ridley records that it was open to visitors on its last Sunday. A smaller house called Binchester Hall is now an old people's home.

WHITWORTH HALL, near Spennymoor

Mark Shafto bought Whitworth in 1652. An 18th century owner was Robert Duncombe Shafto (d.1797), "Bonnie Bobby Shafto". Courtier, man of fashion, he married Anne, daughter and heiress of Thomas Duncombe of Duncombe Park, Yorkshire, and mostly wasted her fortune. His son John left Whitworth to Robert Eden Duncombe Shafto. He rebuilt the Hall c.1820 in a plain style, adding a one-storey wing to house his fine library. His son Robert Duncombe Shafto fought several expensive parliamentary elections: the 1832 contest apparently cost £100,000. Fire destroyed the main Hall in 1876. In 1891 surviving parts were formed into a new house. The Shafto family sold the Hall in the 1980's.

Whitworth Hall (James Dodd, History of Spennymoor, 1897)

HELMINGTON HALL, Willington

Fire destroyed Helmington Hall in 1895: a fragment remains. It was a substantial nine-bay house of c.1687. Entrance and windows had scrolled pediments. The kitchen fireplace had a frieze of four figures — the quarters of the globe — and animals. William Blackett sold Helmington to Ralph Spencer (1736-1805) in 1793. It was "considerably enlarged... by the addition of two handsome Gothic rooms" for his son, the Revd. Robert Spencer (1771-1836). Gardens were "laid out with great taste"; "a new stone bridge" was "lately built". Perhaps an architect and County Bridge Surveyor, Christopher Ebdon (to 1813) or Ignatius Bonomi (from 1813) was responsible? In 1856 Spencer's widow lived at Helmington.

Helmington Hall ruins (J. Davidson)

OLD PARK, Whitworth

Old Park, seat of the Whartons, was extended in Gothick style c.1763, possibly with advice from Thomas Gray (1716-71).

Robert Claxton, the last Claxton owner, died in 1587. Soon after, Old Park was bought by John Wharton (d.1628) of Winston. Thomas Wharton (d.1794), physician, became friendly with Thomas Gray at Pembroke College, Cambridge. On succeeding to Old Park, Wharton made extensive additions. Gray, poet and antiquary, a frequent visitor in the 1760's, might have advised Wharton. He added a drawing room, dining room, semi-octagonal entrance hall, and a fine oak staircase. There were several Gothick window motifs: pointed with Y-tracery, quatrefoils, and elaborate traceried lights in the central, gabled bay.

Thomas Wharton's son Robert succeeded to estates at Grinkle Park, Yorkshire and assumed the name Myddleton. Old Park was mostly occupied by tenants, but Robert's daughter Sophia and her husband, Robert Grey, Vicar of Whitworth (later Bishop of Cape Town), lived there 1834-45. In the 1840's Whitworth Park Colliery opened nearby. Old Park was occupied by Mr. Robson, colliery manager, and then by other tenants. In 1868 Richard Wharton Myddleton's trustees sold Old Park to the Ecclesiastical Commissioners, large landowners in the area.

In 1901 Old Park, "standing in a neglected wilderness in the midst of a bleak colliery district", was demolished by the Commissioners. The tenant "of late years.. had used the noble entrance hall as a store house for farming purposes". Some medieval fragments, pointed and square-headed Gothic windows, were incorporated in a new farmhouse.

Views of Old Park (Newcastle Central Library)

CROOK HALL, Consett

Crook Hall, a late 17th century house, stood north-west of Lanchester, close to the hamlet of Iveston. It was a two-storey, double-pile house of stone, seven bays by five, with elaborate door-cases, quoined corners and a prominent string-course, and originally a high parapet (though photographs suggest that this was later removed). Crook Hall had similarities with the grander Greencroft Hall, Lanchester, and Helmington Hall, Willingdon, both now demolished.

The Shafto family acquired Crook Hall in 1588. About 1640 they sold it to the Baker family. By the 1790's it had ceased to be a Baker seat, and in the French Revolutionary wars it was used as a Roman Catholic seminary for professors and students from Douai, before Ushaw College was opened in 1808. Thereafter Crook Hall was either "deserted" or used as a farmhouse. In the later 19th century nearby Consett sprang up as an iron and steel town, and the Crook Hall Ironworks, a property of the Derwent Iron Company, were opened nearby.

About 1900 Crook Hall was dismantled, and the stone, which was still in good condition, was bought by the historian George Neasham to use in building his own house, West Park near Lanchester.

Crook Hall (Beamish Museum)

STANLEY HALL

No illustration is known of Stanley Hall, described by Mackenzie and Ross (1834) as standing south of Tanfield "on a wild hill top". It was "an old, double, gavel-ended house", that is, a house with wings. By 1834 it belonged to Peregrine Townley of Townley Hall, Lancashire.

Crook Hall (Beamish Museum)

GREENCROFT HALL, Lanchester

"A spacious old mansion... with a southern prospect, commanding a view of Lanchester" (Hutchinson). Greencroft was built c.1670 and given sashes and a pedimented porch in the 18th century. In the early 19th century, one-bay wings were added in the same style.

The Claverings owned Axwell Park, Blaydon, from 1629 and bought Greencroft from Ralph Hall, an impoverished Royalist, in 1670. Sir Thomas Clavering (1791-1853) succeeded in 1794, but lived mostly near Cheltenham, which his French wife preferred. His brother Sir William Clavering (d.1872) succeeded; on Sir William's death Axwell went to his nephew, Sir Henry Clavering, while Greencroft passed to an illegitimate brother, John Clavering (d.1880). John's daughters Clara and Agatha succeeded him. They married Belgians, Baron de Knyff and Baron de Montfaucon. By 1930 the owners were the du Quesnoys, descendants of the Montfaucons and devisees of the Knyffs.

Greencroft's tenants included Joseph Davidson (d.1868), a lavish host. After John Clavering's death, tenants were the Cochranes, coal-owners, Burgoyne Johnson, and Robert Eccles until 1930. The Hall was empty until 1939, when the army took it over. After 1945 it was unoccupied and decayed rapidly. The fittings were sold in 1954 (including white marble Adam-style fireplaces), and Greencroft was demolished in 1960.

To the east was an 18th century Gothick arch and cottages, Greencroft Tower. Subsidence undermined it; it was demolished in 1955. The 18th century stable-block has been re-erected as the visitors' centre at Beamish Museum.

Greencroft Hall (G. Neasham Views of mansions... in the Lanchester and Derwent valleys, 1884)

Greencroft Tower (Beamish Museum)

BROADWOOD HALL, Lanchester

Built in 1875 for Edward Taylor-Smith of Colepike Hall, on the site of an old farmhouse, Broadwood Hall was large but fairly restrained for its date. The architect is not known. Taylor-Smith died in 1888, and the estate was sold to the Penman family, who had it until 1958. In 1960 the estate was sold to Cowies, builders, of Sunderland, the house was demolished, and an "executive home" was built on the site.

Broadwood Hall (G. Neasham, Views of mansions... in the Lanchester and Derwent valleys, 1884)

ESHWOOD HALL, New Brancepeth

The house, large but rather plain, was built in 1874 for the local coal-owner, Henry Heath Cochrane. The 60 acre estate included 20 acres of gardens "with trout ponds and waterfalls, with noble rockeries of red sandstone from Carlisle", rhododendrons and redwoods. All this was originally "barren waste and bog". There were extensive greenhouses, including a "peach house" "fernery" and "vinery", and large dog kennels. The estate was offered for sale in 1926 by Messrs. Cochrane & Co. Ltd., owners of the colliery. The *Darlington and Stockton Times* announced on 20 November 1926 that the hall was to be demolished shortly. This took place in 1930, when Eshwood was replaced by a much smaller house.

Eshwood Hall (J. Jamieson, Durham at the opening of the twentieth century, 1906)

RAVENSWORTH CASTLE, near Gateshead

In 1724 Colonel Liddell built a house flanked by the battlemented curtain walls and two towers of the old castle. This is shown in an engraving by Buck, 1728. In the 1750's it was extensively altered for his nephew "by the advice of the late Ld. Leicester and Mr. Payne". Paine gothicised the south end and added some interior decoration. The Countess of Northumberland described the interior in 1760. "In the middle a good Hall and opposite the Enterance is a handsome staircase, taken off with columns." To the right was a drawing room with "Indian paper", to the left a dining room "the side board taken off with columns." Upstairs was a breakfast room and drawing room, with "Brussels tapestries." Hutchinson too described and illustrated the house in 1794, mentioning the "spacious saloon, staircase and a good dining room." He described Paine's breakfast room as "stuccoed" and the upper room as having "tapestry of Antwerp; at one end... the landscape work is strikingly beautiful, in the style of Poussin."

By 1807 Sir Thomas Liddell (d.1885), Tory, and friend of the Prince of Wales (later Prince Regent and George IV), who created him Lord Ravensworth in 1821, had decided to rebuild Ravensworth in the romantic castle style. Over the next 35 years it grew into one of the grandest Gothic Revival houses in the county (rivalled only by "Radical Jack" Lambton's Lambton Castle), with many towers, suggesting Downton Castle, and a Great Hall and a Long Gallery, recalling William Beckford's Fonthill Abbey. Liddell's employed the royal architect John Nash; though it is not clear

Ravensworth Castle, south front (Gateshead Public Library)

Entrance front (Gateshead Public Library)

West end and conservatory (Gateshead Public Library)

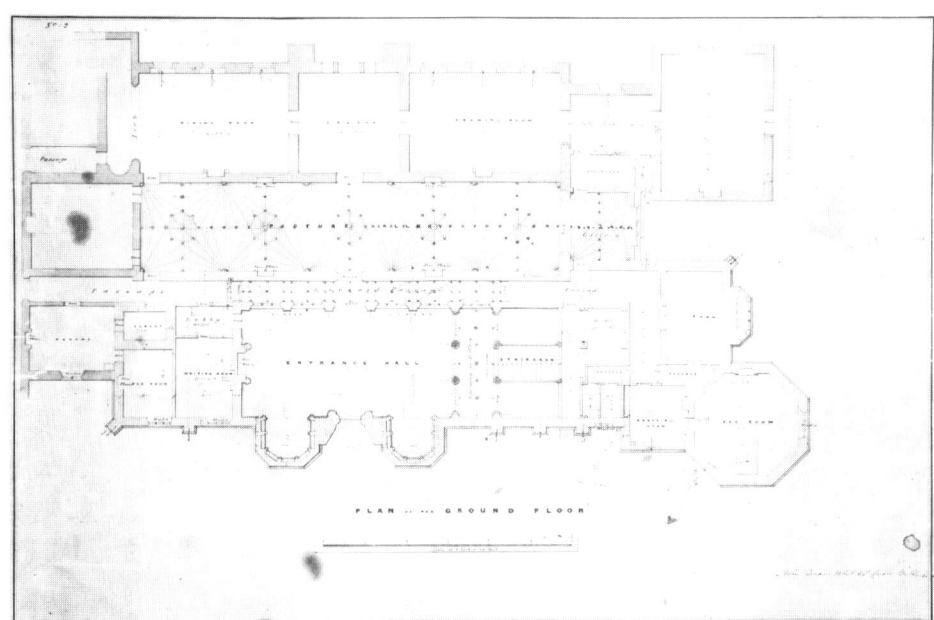

Ground plan by John Nash (British Architectural Library)

what part Liddell himself played in suggesting the design.

The long south front, punctuated at intervals by towers of various shapes and outlines, and containing the state rooms, was probably erected first. From about 1822, Lord Ravensworth's second son Thomas Liddell (1800-56) began to take an interest in the design, and the final disposition of the south front is close to a sketch elevation inscribed by Lord Ravensworth "Plan suggested by Thomas". Lord Ravensworth retired from politics in 1832 to devote his time to building; the *Durham Chronicle* announced (16 May 1840) "the works in progress are very extensive. A great number of hands are employed upon the erection, and it is understood that the original design of the architect is to be forthwith carried into effect." The *Illustrated London News* reported the final completion of the work in 1846. By then the castle had hosted two glittering events, the visit of the Duke of Wellington in 1827, and the coming of age of Ravensworth's grandson in 1841.

The south front continued with a cloister screening offices, and ended in another tower. On the west side Thomas

Drawing room and ante-library (Northumberland Record Office)

another tower. On the west side Thomas The entrance was on the north side. The exteriors gave no hint of the Great Hall into which it opened, cathedralesque, with arcades, tall arched recesses, a hammer-beam roof modelled on Eltham Palace, Surrey, and a double staircase rising to an arched landing framing a statue of St. George and the Dragon. Between the Great Hall and the state rooms ran the Long Gallery, which was fan-vaulted and top-lit by fan-lights, some supporting Gothic lanterns in the manner of Christ Church, Oxford. Here Lord Ravensworth's picture collection hung, including some notable Poussins. The state rooms on the south side, with plastered ceilings and bosses at the intersections, were a less interesting enfilade leading to Thomas Liddell's conservatory.

The 5th Lord Ravensworth died in 1919. In 1920 a sale of furniture and books and pictures (including Rembrandt's "Baptism of the eunuch") took place. The 6th Baron moved to Eslington Park in Northumberland. Ravensworth became a girls' school. The 7th Baron, who succeeded in 1932, decided to demolish the Castle and build a model village. There was an outcry in the press. Lord Ravensworth revealed that a 30-acre coalfield beneath the Castle had undermined it: the foundations were sinking and the walls were cracking. He died in 1950 before the village plan could be achieved, but his successor, assisted by Colonel Stafford, demolished the Castle in 1953 and erected craftsman-built houses. The old towers and parts of the stable still remain.

Ravensworth Castle, Great Hall (Northumberland Record Office)

Great Hall and staircase (Northumberland Record Office)

*South front
(Gateshead Public Library)*

Picture Gallery (Northumberland Record Office)

*Ravensworth Castle
after Paine's alterations
(W. Hutchinson, History of Durham, 1789)*

Picture Gallery (Northumberland Record Office)

GIBSIDE

Gibside has been a roofless shell since 1920, but it still preserves the character of a long, low, Jacobean-style building capped by an exaggeratedly high castellated parapet. The estate was more renowned for its landscape park, created in c.1730-60 by George Bowes, with its banqueting house by Daniel Garrett, its orangery and column of British liberty, and its mausoleum chapel by James Paine (now owned by the National Trust). The estate was until recently the property of the Earl of Strathmore.

Gibside passed from the Marleys, owners from c.1200, to Roger Blakiston of Coxhoe in 1450. His descendant William Blakiston rebuilt the house c.1625. The entrance porch, though reconstructed in 1805, probably represents the 17th century porch, with Tuscan columns on high pedestals, the Royal Arms of James I flanked by sculpted figures (similar to a pair at Chillingham Castle, Northumberland), the initials of William and Jane Blakiston and the date 1620.

On the death of Sir Francis Blakiston in 1713, the estate passed to his daughter Elizabeth, wife of Sir William Bowes of Streatlam Castle, Thus Gibside was added to the Bowes' possessions; in 1722 Sir William's third son George Bowes succeeded. Bowes was M.P. for the county for over 30 years, and was a founder of the "Grand Allies", the great partnership of Durham coal owners. He grew extremely wealthy on coal, and left a fortune of more than £1 million. He devoted much time and money to creating the landscape park at Gibside.

View of Gibside (W. Hutchinson, History of Durham, 1787)

Entrance front (Beamish Museum)

He made few changes to the house, but the north front at the rear, where the ground falls steeply to the River Derwent, was remodelled with sash windows. This was probably the work of Daniel Garrett (d.1753), who was employed on the estate from about 1743, designing (possibly) a Gothick tower in 1743, Palladian stables in 1746, and the Gothick Banqueting House in 1751. This had splendid rococo-Gothick plasterwork, now mostly lost. There is no indication that Garrett designed similar plasterwork for the house, but some remodelling of the rooms probably took place for George Bowes.

Hutchinson described the chief parts as "old, of the architecture which prevailed in the beginning of the seventeenth century", and a plate in his book shows Gibside from the north. The house can be seen to be double-pile, three-storey, with pitched roofs.

George Bowes (d.1760) was succeeded by his daughter, Mary Eleanor. She married (1767) John, 9th Earl of Strathmore. Gibside would pass to the Lyon family, but not before the Countess, whose husband died in 1776, married an impoverished Irish adventurer, Captain Stoney, who took the name Bowes and squandered her money, felled the plantations at Gibside, and in 1787, after his cruelty forced the Countess to apply for court protection, abducted her and tried to make her sign away her property. A sensational ten-day chase by stage-coach ended in his arrest and imprisonment.

Mary Eleanor, the "unhappy Countess" died in 1800. Gibside and Streatlam passed to her son, John, 10th Earl of Strathmore, on his coming-of-age in 1790.

(1) Entrance (Gateshead Public Library)
(2) West front (RCHM England)
(3) North end, offices (RCHM England)

He completed the unfinished mausoleum chapel in 1812, replanted the woods, and reconstructed the house in 1805. His architect, recommended by Lord Delaval for work at Ford Castle, Northumberland, was the Berwickshire masterbuilder Alexander Gilkie (c.1756-1834). The date 1805 is carved on the front porch. The house was reduced to two storeys, and the large service wing was presumably added then. The rambling composition was tied together by the overwhelming castellated parapet. In 1813 John Dobson made designs for an ambitious conservatory adjoining the house in a similar castellated manner. This was not executed, but his drawings of Gibside provide evidence for its appearance and plan at that date.

The 10th Earl married, just before his death in 1820, Mary Milner, who had been his mistress for many years. Their son John Bowes (1811-85) inherited the Durham and Yorkshire estates but not the earldom. He lived at Streatlam Castle, and founded the Bowes Museum. His mother lived on at Gibside with her second husband until her death in 1860. Afterwards Gibside was little used. On the death of John Bowes in 1885 the estates were left to the Earl of Strathmore. In 1889 there were plans for a hydropathic establishment. Occasional picnics at Gibside (recalled by Queen Elizabeth the Queen Mother) were taken by the Bowes-Lyon family in the early 20th century. Land army girls were billeted in the house in the 1914-18 war, but by then its roof was failing and it lacked plumbing and sanitation. It was gutted in 1920, and a large fireplace, with terms of Hercules and Samson supporting a large mantel decorated with Blakiston arms, was installed in the billiard room at Glamis Castle.

Fireplace, now at Glamis Castle (The Bowes Museum)

Banqueting House, plasterwork now lost (The Bowes Museum)

BRADLEY HALL, Wolsingham

Bradley Hall, east of Wolsingham, was ruinous when Hutchinson wrote in 1794. His plate shows an old moated manor house, built in the 15th century by the Eures of Witton Castle, and embellished in the late 16th century with two bay-windows raised on tunnel vaults and joined by a double arch. There were steps on each side of the bays, and the centre was an open loggia. By 1794 Bradley was the property of Thomas Bowes of Gibside and Streatlam. The Elizabethan work has gone, but some remains are incorporated in a farmhouse, and more stand as ruins.

Bradley Hall (W. Hutchinson, History of Durham, 1787)

CONSETT HALL

Little seems known of the history of Consett Hall, south-west of the town, a house mentioned by Surtees (1820). In 1841 Consett Iron Works was established, and Consett Hall was linked with it. In 1856 the manager, George Foster, lived at Consett Hall, and in 1884 William Jenkins, manager, was the occupant. Photographs suggest that the Hall was substantially rebuilt about 1850, probably in white brick, with square-headed Gothic windows.

Consett Hall (Beamish Museum)

RYTON HOUSE

A curious house with seemingly little known history. Ryton was an 18th century building of brick, the main front of two storeys, the sides of three, in an awkward juxtaposition, shown clearly in the somewhat naïve engraving by Boniface Muss. At the corner was a confusion of Venetian doors and windows and a lunette, at different levels. In the 19th century a bay-window was built out at the side. In one room the Ryton Petty Sessions were held.

To the side of the house was the stable-block, with a tall entrance-arch and facade, an interesting essay in 18th century Gothick, with battlements, cross-slits and panels of quatrefoils and lozenges, symmetrical but very elementary.

The house was latterly a Conservative club; amazingly, and somewhat grotesquely, the main entrance was covered by a shallow greenhouse (it could not be dignified with the name conservatory).

Ryton House, which stood south of the church, was demolished in the 1960's and replaced by an estate of houses. Ryton was the seat of the Humble family in the 18th century. Joseph Lamb (d.1800) married the Humble heiress, and their son Humble Lamb (d.1844) inherited the estate. He was succeeded by his son Joseph Chatto Lamb (1803-84) and grandson Joseph Lamb.

Boniface Muss, Views in Newcastle, c.1790 (Newcastle Central Library)

Ryton House (RCHM England)

Ryton House, c.1900 (J. Davidson)

WINLATON HALL

Once a seat of the Roman Catholic Hodgsons of Hebburn, Winlaton passed c.1700 to Sir William Blackett, who leased it to Sir Ambose Crowley, Tyneside industrialist (d.1713). In 1704 Crowley used the Hall as a chapel, later as a house, offices and warehouse. It was vacated in 1753. Crowley probably added the curious façade of battlemented corner-towers wth a Dutch gable between. An inscribed gable stone read "Crowley and Belts Castle 1864" (Two Belt sisters sold provisions in part of it c.1830). Part of the Hall in domestic use was described as "well-situated, fit for a gentleman's family... with several houses and smith's shops." Joseph Laycock came to Winlaton in the early 18th century to manage Crowley's works. His grandson Joseph Laycock (1798-1881) rebuilt the residential part of the Hall c.1835, but later moved to Low Gosforth House. In 1896 the Hall was the seat of H. W. Grace; it was later owned by Matthew Kirsop, but was demolished in 1928.

Ryton House, entrance to stable yard (RCHM England)

Winlaton Hall (Gateshead Public Library)

STELLA HALL, Blaydon

Stella Hall stood near the Tyne. A former convent of Benedictine nuns, it passed into the hands of the Tempests, merchants of Newcastle, in the late 16th century. The house was built soon after 1600 by Nicholas Tempest. It consisted of a centre and two wings. Its 17th century origin was most evident at the rear, where there was a long wing with mullioned and transomed windows. The family was Roman Catholic, and the house was supposed to have secret rooms to hide priests. A succession of chaplains is recorded from 1688.

Jane Tempest (d.1714), sister and heiress of Sir Francis Tempest (d.1698), married the Roman Catholic William, 4th Lord Widdrington. He joined the 1715 Rebellion, and was condemned to death and his lands were confiscated. Later he was pardoned, and his lands were restored to his family in 1733. He died in 1745.

James Paine was commissioned by his son, Henry, 5th Lord Widdrington (d.1774) to make alterations. He altered the windows of the entrance front, adding Venetian windows in arched frames, and pedimented windows on the first floor. Inside he designed the decoration of the hall, drawing room and library. The hall was a long room screened at each end with ionic columns. The coved ceiling had rococo plasterwork. The library had a screen of fluted Doric columns with a frieze of triglyphs and paterae above. The most exuberant plasterwork was in the drawing room, with swags and garlands, an oval niche framed with palms, and a framed landscape in plaster with a shooting star (in allusion to Stella).

On the death of the 5th Lord Widdrington the Stella and Stanley estates passed by bequest to Peregrine Towneley

Stella Hall (University of Newcastle upon Tyne)

Rear view (RCHM England)

of Towneley, Lancashire, and the Hall was usually occupied by tenants, in 1834 by Mrs. Bridget Dunn (the Dunns were local coal-owners), and in 1856 by John D. Lambton. The estate was sold in 1850 to Sir Joseph Cowen (1800-73), industrialist and Chairman of the River Tyne Improvement Commissioners for 20 years. His son Joseph Cowen (1829-1900), radical politician, formed the Northern Reform League in 1858, espoused Christian Democracy, and was friendly with European reformers such as Garibaldi, Orsini, Mazzini and Kossuth, some of whom were entertained at Stella.

Joseph Cowen's daughter Jane Cowen lived at Stella until 1946. She was well-known for charitable work for the poor and handicapped. She left Stella to the University of Durham. It was demolished in 1953 for a housing estate.

Views of the drawing room, Stella Hall (Gateshead Public Library)

Stella Hall, small dining room (Gateshead Public Library)

ELVASTON HALL, Ryton
PARK HEAD HALL, Winlaton

At Ryton was Elvaston Hall, called in 1896 "a large modern stone mansion", home for some years of Sir Charles Parsons (1854-1931), inventor of the steam turbine for ships. No illustration of it has been found. Park Head Hall (originally Derwent Villa), Winlaton, called by Fordyce "a pleasantly situated mansion, in the Elizabethan style of architecture", was built in 1836, and was the seat of George Heppel Ramsay (1790-1879), industrialist. His mother was descended from German steelmakers who came to the Derwent in the 17th century. Ramsay was succeeded by his son John T. Ramsay and grandson G. R. Ramsay.

Stella Hall, entrance (Gateshead Public Library)

Stella Hall, library (Gateshead Public Library)

FARNACRES, Gateshead

Farnacres, south-west of Gateshead in the Team Valley, passed to the Liddells of Ravensworth in 1671. In the 18th century it was the home of Nicholas Watson (d.1795), their bailiff. 19th and early 20th century tenants were the Revd. R. H. Williamson, John Barras, brewer, Mark Archer, Dunston engineer, and F. W. Bernard, the "Low Fell Giant", the last occupant. It was a long house with a sweeping verandah, and boasted a "museum", presumably for stuffed birds, rocks and minerals. From the 1930's the Team Valley Trading estate encroached more and more, and Farnacres was demolished in the 1960's.

Farnacres (Newcastle Central Lbrary)

BIRTLEY HALL

Apparently designed by John Dobson for J. Warwick in 1843, Birtley was a plain stone house in a wooded estate, overlooking Birtley Iron Works. Many owners were managers of the works, including G. Skipsey in 1828, Benjamin Thompson in 1834, John Hine Hunt in 1851 and Edward Perkins (1821-71) in 1865. (In 1834 Frederick Perkins of Southwark leased Birtley Iron Company for 60 years; in 1858 Edward Perkins became a partner). Perkins made many alterations. His son Charles moved to Northumberland. In 1906 the occupant was Herbert Fenwick, Charles Perkins' son-in-law. The last occupant was Henry Angus Murton. Birtley was demolished c.1916.

Birtley Hall (Gateshead Central Library)

GATESHEAD PARK HOUSE

The shell of Gateshead Park, which was gutted by fire in 1891, survives in a much-altered and barely recognisable form as a factory building. It was a distinguished 18th century house mostly rebuilt to designs of James Gibbs in 1730-33.

The Park estate was the Bishop of Durham's park in Gateshead, but by the 17th century it was leased to the lord of the manor. William Cotesworth became lord of the manor in 1716, improved the agricultural land, let out the river frontage for industries such as foundries, glass and chemical works and roperies, and increased the rental revenue considerably. Later, collieries were established on the estate.

Cotesworth rebuilt old Park House (a remnant of which might have survived in the low wing with a Dutch gable) in 1723. In 1729-33 the house was greatly enlarged for Cotesworth's son-in-law Henry Ellison by the architect James Gibbs. It was a brick house with stone dressings, two-and-a-half storeys, and a typical Gibbsian doorcase on the garden side. It had a fine elevated site overlooking the Tyne, nearly opposite Newcastle. A drawing of the stone staircase, and some of Gibbs' ceiling designs, with alternatives by Paulo Franchini, are the only known records of the interior.

The Ellisons built Hebburn Hall in 1790 and made it their main residence. In 1825 Park House was leased to Isaac Cookson, junior, and other industrialists followed: Charles Bulmer, Alexander Grey, and Henry and Alfred Allhusen. The estate passed into the hands of the Ecclesiastical Commissioners in 1857, and much of it was sold for building land. Park House was acquired by the firm of Clarke

Gateshead Park, by W. Davison, 1830 (J. Davidson)

Gateshead Park, by W. H. Knowles (Gateshead Public Library)

Chapman in 1884 and converted into offices. In November 1891 it was burnt down and its remains became an industrial building. It is still owned by the firm of NEI Clark Chapman.

There was a painting of Park House by Richardson, formerly owned by Hugh Lee Pattison of Scots Houses, sold by auction in 1887. In 1922 one of the Allhusens offered £5 for information on its whereabouts.

Gateshead Park, staircase, by W. H. Knowles (Gateshead Public Library)

DECKHAM'S HALL, Gateshead

A small Gateshead estate, named after its owner in 1614, Thomas Deckham. No illustration is known. The Hall stood on high ground above Gateshead. It passed through various hands, including William Cotesworth (of Park House). A colliery was worked on the estate from the 18th century to 1890. The Hall was offered for sale in 1809, and bought in 1817 by William James, who substantially rebuilt it. In 1858 it was sold to Benjamin Biggar, a Newcastle merchant. He sold it in 1873, and various tenants occupied it until it was demolished in 1930. Much of the estate was sold off for building from 1882; the east part became council housing in the 1920's and 1930's.

Gateshead Park, factory building (RCHM England)

REDHEUGH HALL, Gateshead

Redheugh was an old house on the bank of the River Tyne, held of the Bishop of Durham since the 13th century by the Redheugh family. It passed to the Whites, in 1619 to the Liddells, and in 1748 it was bought by Adam Askew of Newcastle, physician, for his son Henry Askew. The Askews held the estate until the 1870's. Redheugh was often tenanted.

It was a late 17th century house, enlarged in the mid-18th century, probably by the Askews, with two wings. A pedimented porch was added in the centre, and Venetian windows in the wings. There is no plan of the interior, but a fine doorcase of c.1760 in the drawing room, with a richly carved cornice supported on consoles, was illustrated in *The Architect* in 1912.

Redheugh's setting was spoilt by running the Newcastle and Carlisle railway between the house and the river in the 1830's. In 1835 Adam Askew, grandson of the earlier Adam Askew, leased Redheugh to William Cuthbert of Newcastle, glass manufacturer, and moved south. Although the railway was moved in 1839, the estate was put up for sale in 1850, offering building plots for villas for Newcastle men. It was unsold until 1871, when the opening of Redheugh Bridge across the Tyne increased accessibility from Newcastle. Much land was sold for house-building, and the Hall stood empty. In 1912 it was a storehouse: the 18th century drawing room held hay. The house was owned latterly by Redheugh Colliery Company.

A bad fire in 1920 left it roofless. The ruins remained until 1936, when they were demolished by members of the International Voluntary Service for Peace.

Redheugh Hall (Gateshead Public Library)

Redheugh Hall, on the banks of the Tyne, by William Beilby (The Duke of Northumberland)

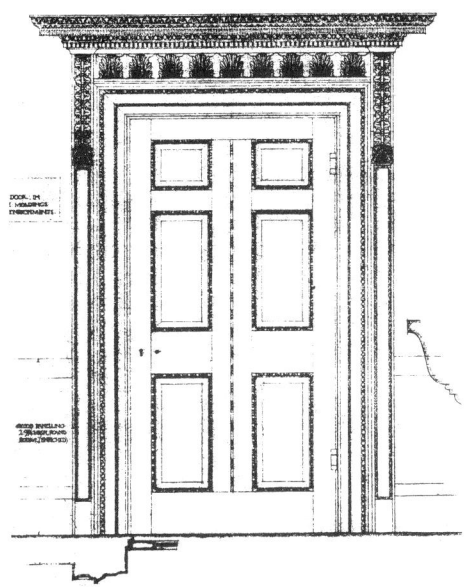

*Drawing room doorway
(The Architect, 30 August 1912)*

Redheugh Hall (Gateshead Public Library)

SHERIFF HILL HALL, Gateshead

The enclosure of Gateshead Fell was completed in 1822, and there was a rapid increase in population soon after. Sheriff Hill Hall, a substantial stone-built villa, was built about 1828 for Matthew Plummer. It was a block of fine ashlar, with a central porch of two Ionic columns *in antis*, conventional sash-windows and a heavy parapet. From its position on the edge of the hill, wrote Mackenzie and Ross (1834) the view embraced "the whole line of the Tyne, the beautiful vale of Ravensworth, the city of Durham, and the German Ocean both to the north and the east."

Sheriff Hill Hall (Gateshead Public Library)

SALTWELL HALL, Gateshead

The Saltwellside estate was in the Team valley. The house was perhaps late 16th or early 17th century. Drawings show it with two large bay-windows. Photographs show that most of the old external features were gradually lost.

The 16th century owners were the Hedworths of Harraton; 17th century owners were the Halls and Maddisons. In 1750 it passed to Joseph Liddell of Moorhouse, Carlisle, who had interests in the Gateshead Fell collieries. In 1792 Saltwell was sold to Joseph Dunn, who (c.1805) split up the estate, retaining the Hall and 110 acres. From 1850 Saltwell Hall was occupied by Charles Bulmer of the Tyne Iron Company, from 1893 by John Rowell, brewer. Hs widow was the last occupant. In 1903 much land was sold for Saltwell cemetery, and the Hall became an isolation hospital. It was demolished in 1936.

Saltwell Hall, by Ewbank (Durham Dean & Chapter Longstaffe MSS)

SALTWELL TOWERS

William Wailes, Newcastle stained-glass artist, bought part of Saltwellside, and in 1856 designed the spectacular Gothic Saltwell Towers (built 1860-71). Of red brick with black and yellow decoration, it was Elizabethan in style, the skyline punctuated by dramatic towers, turrets and pinnacles. In 1876 Wailes (d.1881) sold Saltwell Towers to Gateshead, but leased it back. A later occupant was J. A. D. Shipley (d.1909), whose picture collection became the Shipley Art Gallery, Gateshead. In 1914-18 Saltwell Towers was a hospital, but afterwards stood empty until used as the Local and Industrial Museum, 1933-68- Dry rot forced its closure, and it has been derelict and threatened with total demolition since then.

Saltwell Hall (Gateshead Public Library)

Saltwell Towers (Beamish Museum)

WHITE HOUSE, Heworth

On a hill above Heworth, with views of the Tyne and Wear estuaries, White House was of no particular style or character, with gables and wings added haphazardly. A sundial on the south side was dated 1680. White House was a leasehold estate under the Church of Durham. In the 17th century it was owned by of the Jennisons, staunch Roman Catholics; in the late 17th century it was bought by Edward Colville, Newastle butcher, grazier and importer, whose daughter married Lord Ossulton, later Earl of Tankerville. It passed to John Stafford of Monkwearmouth, and in 1820 Richard Carnaby Foster, his son and grandson. They had interests in farming, quarrying, shipping and coal. By 1900 the house was threatened by the encroachment of Heworth Colliery pit-heap. The last occupant, to 1938, was Thomas Maltby Clague, chemist and antiquary. In 1939-45 it was used to store potatoes and turnips. In 1957 the Church Commissioners sold it to Felling Council for the Leam Lane estate; by 1960 it was derelict, and was demolished soon after.

White House, Heworth (RCHM England)

White House (RCHM England)

THOMPSON'S HALL, South Shields

Major Thompson lived here in 1819, at which time it was called Hill House. To add to the confusion it is also occasionally referred to as High Hall. Whatever its name, it must have ranked among the very best domestic buildings in Georgian South Shields. It was one of several sizeable houses on the riverside, home to master mariners involved in the coal trade to London. It degenerated into tenements with the addition of a further storey and suffered the added indignity of a beer shop in the side elevation.

The house was demolished to make way for a road scheme. A photograph dated 18th April 1939 shows a section of the upper floor flying through the air complete with classical fireplace.

Thompson's Hall (South Tyneside Libraries)

WESTOE HOUSE, South Shields

Westoe House stood at the head of the village and was first recorded in 1753. At that time it was owned by Robert Walker, a shipping butcher from Newcastle who had made his fortune in the Greenland fisheries boom.

A seventeenth century house was incorporated in the north eastern corner. Robert Ingham, the first M.P. for South Shields, inherited it in 1825. Before his death in 1875 most of the estate had been sold and the building was altered by its late nineteenth century owner, Matthew Cay, a shipowner. The last private owner died in 1943 and the Ingham Infirmary bought it but never used it. In 1958 "deserted, derelict and beyond repair" it was demolished.

Westoe House (South Tyneside Libraries)

SIMONSIDE HALL,
South Shields

Robert Wallis challenged the might of the Corporation of Newcastle and their monopoly on shipbuilding on the Tyne by opening the first shipyard in South Shields in about 1720. His country seat was at Simonside but it was after his death that his second son John built or rebuilt Simonside Hall in 1784. Contemporaries remarked on its fine views of Jarrow Slake. The battlemented front parapet and rear tower must have been nineteenth century additions, perhaps by Henry Major. South Shields A. F. C. took a lease on the whole site in 1947. One wing had already disappeared when the main block went in about 1973.

Simonside Hall (RCHM England)

CLEADON COTTAGE,
South Shields

"It is not beautiful, it is not even distinguished. It is not elegantly detailed nor of fine proportions. It is neither an exciting building nor impressive. It lacks elegance, comfort and charm" said architect Peter Elphick at the enquiry into the demolition of Cleadon Cottage. His words helped to seal the fate of the house, which was demolished in 1982. It was built by Robert Swinburne, a glass manufacturer, in 1853 and has been attributed to John Dobson. Forty years later James Kirkley carried out major works including a vast palm house. Sunderland Corporation bought it in 1918 and from 1921 to 1978 it was used as a hospital.

Cleadon Cottage (South Tyneside Libraries)

WHITBURN HALL

Whitburn Hall, a long, rambling building containing work of several different periods, became the seat of the Williamson family after the destruction of Monkwearmouth Hall by fire in 1790.

The oldest part, at the east end, had 17th century windows with hood-moulds. Next was a long, plain 18th century wing of six bays. About 1800 a complicated nine-bay-section was added, one bay projecting as a small wing, with a Venetian window. This part was remodelled (by John Dobson) in 1856, and again c.1880, for Sir Hedworth Williamson, in a neo-Baroque style. An extraordinary three-bay cast iron balcony, supported by caryatids, was added. The windows above were heightened, and higher still were *oeil-de-boeuf* windows and a balustrade with urns. In the 1930's, when Chesterfield House, London, was being broken up and demolished, the panelling and decorations of the French Room, c.1750 by Isaac Ware, were acquired and installed at Whitburn. They have since been installed at the Bowes Museum, Barnard Castle.

Whitburn Hall was burnt in 1978 and demolished in 1980.

Whitburn Hall (RCHM England)

(2) Central section, with caryatid balcony (RCHM England)
(3) First floor room, ceiling (RCHM England)

USWORTH HOUSE (PEARETH HALL) Washington

William Peareth (d.1775), Clerk of the Chamber and Alderman of Newcastle for 50 years, built Usworth House to the west of Great Usworth in about 1750. The grounds were presided over by a large 3 storey canted bay containing the principal apartments. The entrance front was of seven bays, the central three of which were slightly projected to relieve the facade, an effect also achieved by the detailing round the front door and the window above. The composition was completed by two storey pavilions. Generally known as Peareth Hall, perhaps to distinguish it from Little Usworth Hall, the house was in the late nineteenth century the home of John Bailey, wine merchant. It was demolished some time between 1895 and 1919. One wing survives.

Usworth House, garden front (Newcastle Central Library)

LITTLE USWORTH HALL

An old manor house with square-headed Gothic windows, stood near Manor House Farm between New Washington and Usworth Colliery. Demolished c.1910 as unfit for occupation. A drawing from an old print, is the only record known.

Usworth House, entrance front (E. Kennewell)

NORTH BIDDICK HALL, Washington

Demolished in 1966 in the expansion of Washington new town. Despite its apparent 19th century exterior, it was an old house with work from the 16th century onwards. Some rooms were panelled, in an early 18th century style. The rich ceiling decoration was probably 19th century. The estate belonged to various families, the Hyltons of Hylton Castle, the Carrs of Cocken Hall, and then the Davison family. In 1856 the estate belonged to Joseph Cook, of Messrs. J. and C. Cook, "iron-founders, spade and shovel makers." It was still the seat of Joseph Cook in 1894.

North Biddick Hall (RCHM England)

Venetian window on staircase, panelling of ground floor room, a ceiling detail (RCHM England)

HERRINGTON HALL, Sunderland

Herrington Hall stood in Middle Herrington and its cellars were dated 1570. Despite this, the building in its final form probably dated from about 1795 when, after many generations, the Robinsons sold it to William Beckwith. Although retaining its ownership, General Beckwith soon moved to the Silksworth House Estate, inherited by his wife Priscilla. Later it was bought by the Earls of Durham and for most of the nineteenth century it was let to a succession of tenants. In the twentieth century the Vaux family rented it but the last occupant was Mr. Harry Bell, a local builder. In 1947 it was bought by the Miners Welfare Commission for use as a rehabilitation centre but this never materialised and the National Coal Board demolished it in 1957.

Herrington Hall (Sunderland Echo)

THORNHILL HOUSE, Sunderland

Rarely can the external architectural features of a house have been so well and truly concealed by ivy as at Thornhill House. South west of Sunderland, it was built and possibly designed by a self-made man in the shipping and timber trades, John Thornhill, once described as "a curious mixture of piety, public spirit, conceit and fraud". He moved from Coronation Street, having bought the farm and estate known as Plenty Hall in 1768. The house was the subject of major nineteenth century additions, probably by Sir James Laing who bought the house in 1867. It was demolished in the 1930s and developed for housing, although the lodge of C1810 remains.

Thornhill House (Tyne & Wear Museums)

HYLTON CASTLE, Sunderland

The shell of medieval Hylton Castle still stands, a tall tower-house with four buttress-turrets on its west side, and one wide tower on the east. The central west turrets are linked by a high arch, the elaborate cusping of which fell in 1882. Many coats of arms and heraldic emblems are carved on the west front, and the heraldic evidence dates Hylton to c.1410. The Hyltons were one of the oldest Durham families: the builder of the Castle was probably William de Hylton (1376-1435).

John Hylton (1699-1746) was the last Hylton in the male line. He succeeded his father in 1712. He extended the Castle considerably, giving it north and south wings, and added external Gothic details and internal plasterwork. A survey of the estate by Joseph Roper, 1750, described Hylton as "an ancient Castle, towering between modern built wings". Samuel and Nathaniel Buck's engraving (1728) showed the north wing only, its sash windows with alternate triangular and segmental broken pediments, and an elegant new doorway crowned by a pediment charged with the Hylton arms, approached by a semicircular staircase. Many of the windows of the old tower had been similarly replaced.

After 1728 a matching south wing was added, and it was presumably then that the north-west turret, which had been round, was remodelled to match the others (and the new door was removed). The next phase was Gothick. From similarity with work at Gibside and Raby Castle, this work has been ascribed to Daniel Garrett (d.1753). The door and arch on the west side were covered by a pretty porch with clustered columns,

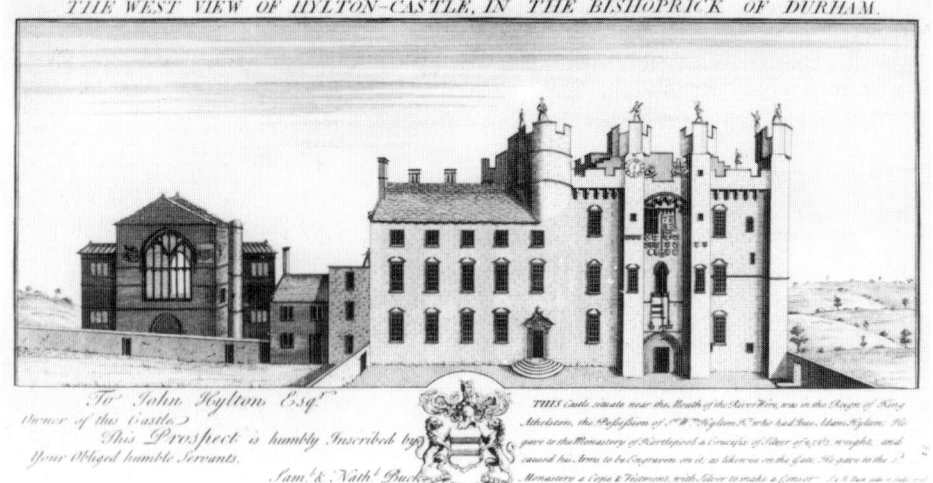

Hylton Castle by Samuel and Nathaniel Buck, 1728

Hylton Castle c.1800 (Newcastle Central Library)

quatrefoil arches and an openwork parapet above. On the east side were single-storey bow-fronted rooms with Gothic windows, linked by a screen of Gothic arches.

Inside, the drawing room and wine room were given decorative plasterwork by Pietro La Franchini (according to an early 19th century source). Franchini worked for Garrett elsewhere in the North. William Howitt described the rooms in *Visits to remarkable places* (1842): they had "stuccoed ceilings, with figures, busts on the walls, and one large scene which seemed to be Venus and Cupid, Apollo fiddling to the gods, Minerva in her helmet, and an old king".

Hylton's niece and heiress Eleanor Hedworth married Sir Richard Musgrave (later Hylton). In 1758 Sir Richard Hylton sold 'Castle Farm' to Mrs. Bowes, widow of George Bowes of Gibside. The Bowes family do not seem to have occupied it. Later in the 18th century the wings were given battlements, perhaps when, late in the 18th century, it was leased to Simon Temple. He restored it and furnished it richly and laid out the gardens and grounds, "hanging woods and ornamental plantations, in long extended avenues" (Hutchinson). Temple's business eventually failed, and in 1819 Hylton passed to Thomas Wade. By 1834 it was unoccupied. When Howitt visited (1842) it was "a scene of great desolation.. the windows for the most part, all along the front, are boarded up.. the whole of this large old house is now empty.. and in the most desolate state". (But a poor family occupied part of the kitchen range). In January 1856 (according to the *Durham Chronicle*), it was burnt down while in the occupation of Mr. Maclaren, a farmer.

The Bowes family sold the estate in

Rear view (Gentleman's Magazine, March 1821)

Rear view, c.1870 (Proceedings of the Society of Antiquaries of Newcastle, 4th series, vol.3 p.328)

1862 to William Briggs of Sunderland. He demolished the wings and replaced the sash-windows of the old Castle with arched windows filled with plate glass. Garrett's west porch was removed, though his eastern work was allowed to remain. The interior was virtually gutted and modern rooms were created.

After Brigg's death in 1871 his son Colonel Charles J. Briggs succeeded, and after his death the Castle was purchased about 1908 by the Monkwearmouth Colliery Company. It stood empty for many years, and the lead was stolen from the roof. Housing estates gradually surrounded it, and it was reduced to a shell and passed into the care of the Ministry of Works. The successor organisation, English Heritage, now maintains it.

FORD HALL, Sunderland

George Mowbray built Ford Hall in 1785 on land acquired by his father, Teasdale Mowbray, from the Hiltons of Hylton Castle. Six years later George Mowbray and his son sold it to John Goodchild for £14,500. Goodchild lived on the adjoining Pallion Estate and let the house to the Havelock family.

Their son Henry, born at Ford in 1795, was destined to become General Havelock, the hero of Lucknow. John Goodchild's bank failed in 1816 and the house passed to the Fenwick family. Their descendants agreed a sale of the hall and 174 acres to the Corporation of Sunderland in 1924. By this time it had been vacant for 20 years and the Corporation demolished it.

Front, c.1900 (J. Jamieson, Durham at the opening of the 20th Century, 1906)

Ford Hall (Tyne & Wear Museums Service)

PALLION, Sunderland

The unusual name is said to be a contraction of Pavilion, the summer seat of the Lords of Dalden. Down by the river, it remained a rural retreat until Sunderland's encroachments led to its demolition in 1901. The site was later developed for industry.

The nineteenth century house replaced an earlier hall and it stood four square with plain stone elevations. George Short, the shipbuilder, was there from 1850 and it was the birthplace of Sir Joseph Wilson Swann, the inventor of the incandescent light bulb.

The stairs and many other fittings were removed to Unthank Hall in Northumberland.

Pallion (Tyne & Wear Museums Service)

LOW BARNES, Sunderland

The Barnes Estate on the Durham Road was split in 1668. Low Barnes was bought by the Pemberton Family in 1783 and it remained in their ownership until the 1920s, when it was acquired to make Barnes Park. The house in its final form was in the classical style with stuccoed brickwork and pilasters. It was built or remodelled for the family in the 19th century and has been attributed to Thomas Moore, the architect of Ashbrooke Hall. By the end of the 19th century the Pembertons no longer lived there and it was let to a laundry company. In 1921 it was demolished and a bowling green was laid out on the site. Gate piers and a derelict cottage survive.

High Barnes, the home of the Ettricke family, was rebuilt in 1778 and demolished in 1900.

Low Barnes (Tyne & Wear Museums Service)

ASHBROOKE (CORBY) HALL
Sunderland

Described by at least one writer as one of the finest houses ever built in Sunderland, this large Italianate villa of 1864 lent its name to the lush Ashbrooke area of Sunderland, where its lodge may still be seen. The architect was Thomas Moore, also responsible for Monkwearmouth Station. His client was James Hartley MP, the famous glassmaker. On Hartley's death in 1886 it was acquired by John Short, of Short Brothers, ship builders and timber merchants. His wife lived there until her death in 1932.

A large port-cochere led to a most sumptuous interior with very heavy decorative plasterwork forming an extravaganza from floor to ceiling and back down again the other side. The apsidal hall, with stained glass, was later converted into a chapel by the Jesuits, who bought Ashbrooke from the executors in 1932 and converted it into a retreat house for men. They renamed it Corby Hall after Ralph Corby, a Jesuit martyr who was hanged in London after a preliminary trial in Sunderland. In 1973 this use was discontinued and after a well documented period of dereliction it was demolished in 1976.

Ashbrooke Hall (RCHM England)

The central hall (RCHM England)

HARRATON HALL,
Chester-le-Street

Harraton Hall occupied the site of Lambton Castle, on the north banks of the River Wear. Confusingly, the Lambton family estates and Lambton House (demolished 1797) were on the opposite bank. Harraton, anciently a seat of the D'Arcys, had by the 17th century passed to the Hedworths. Sir John Hedworth (d.1642) leased his estates and mines improvidently, and was forced to leave Harraton. His son John (d.1655) saw his estates sequestrated and granted away during the Commonwealth. His son John Hedworth (d.1688) retrieved the estates and finances. It was probably for him that Harraton Hall was rebuilt, as shown in a painting. It was a five-bay, two-storey house with a balustraded parapet and another balustrade atop the hipped roof with dormer windows. The main windows were late 17th century cross-windows with segmental pediments. The painting also shows the coal-staiths in the busy River Wear below the Hall.

John Hedworth had two daughters. The elder, Dorothy, married Ralph Lambton; the younger married Sir William Williamson of Monkwearmouth. In 1714 Ralph Lambton bought Williamson's share of the Harraton lands, thus re-uniting the estate.

A plate in *Vitruvius Britannicus*, 1716, though specifically marked 'Chester-le-Street' and 'John Hedworth', should refer to The Deanery (q.v.), but actually looks more like a plan for remodelling Harraton Hall in Palladian style by Colen Campbell. If so, it was never executed.

Harraton Hall, c.1700, painting.

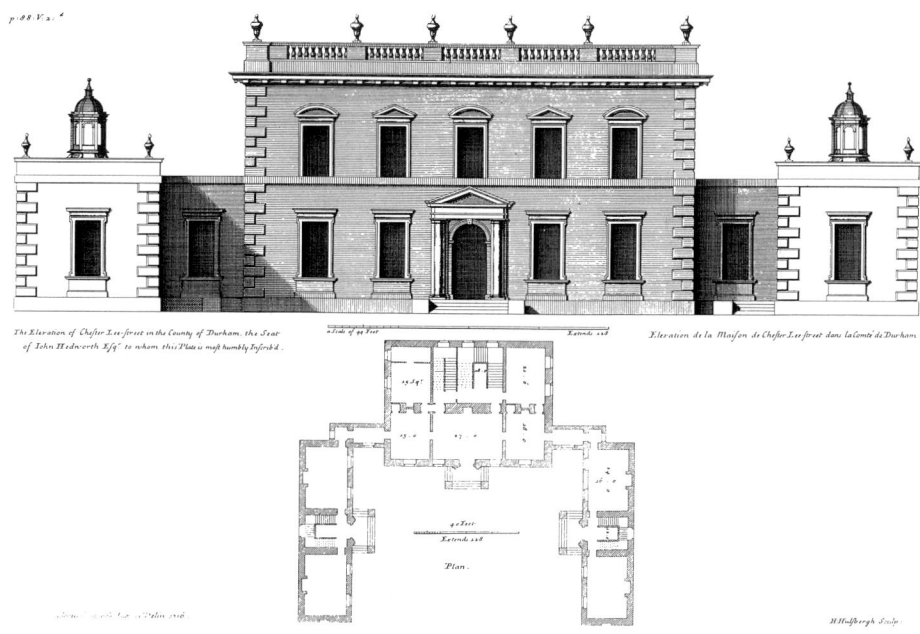

*'Chester-le-Street' for 'John Hedworth'
(C. Campbell, Vitruvius Britannicus, ii. 1716, pl.88)*

LAMBTON CASTLE

Although large parts of Lambton Castle still stand, the romantic castle of the 1820's, designed by Ignatius Bonomi for 'Radical Jack' Lambton, the 1st Earl of Durham, and enlarged still further in the 1860's by John Dobson and Sidney Smirke, was drastically reduced in 1932.

The Lambtons acquired the Harraton Hall estate from the Hedworths in 1688. About a century later, General John Lambton (1710-94) conceived the idea of building a great neoclassical house, Lambton Hall, on the site of Harraton Hall. His son William Henry Lambton (1765-97) commissioned the architect Joseph Bonomi (1739-1808) to make designs, but Lambton's death brought the project to an end. Bonomi was retained, however, by the trustees of his son, John George Lambton (1792-1840), and between 1796 and 1802 created a substantial house in the 'Adam' castle style, towering above the River Wear. The exterior of Lambton Hall is shown in an engraving in Surtees' *Durham*, 1816, and the neoclassical interiors were illustrated in paintings by Bonomi shown at the Royal Academy in 1800-02.

This neoclassical work was swept away, and the Hall was transformed into Lambton Castle in the 1820's for John George Lambton, 1st Earl of Durham, by Bonomi's son Ignatius Bonomi (1789-1870), the Durham architect. Lambton was possibly inspired by Lord Ravensworth's nearby castle, and there is a record of him and Bonomi inspecting Brancepeth Castle in 1822. Lambton Castle, high above the Wear, had the advantage of a more spectacular site; and Bonomi exploited it to the full. He kept the shell of his father's Hall, romanticised it with battlements, towers turrets, a cloister

Lambton Castle, south-east view (D. Sherburn)

Bird's-eye view by Ignatius Bonomi (J. Scovil)

and pinnacles, and continued the Castle along a vast terrace constructed above the steep river valley. He cleverly embellished a wing with flying buttresses, and terminated the facade with an octagonal tower based on Guy's Tower at Warwick Castle.

In the time of the 2nd Earl, the Castle foundations, which had been built over old coal workings, began to fail, and the Castle was threatened with collapse. Bonomi, who had retired from practice, was unfairly blamed for bad design. The task of shoring up the building was given to Bonomi's Newcastle colleague John Dobson. More than £35,000 was spent on filling up the old seams and stabilising the foundations. In 1860-65 part of the Castle was dismantled and replaced (at a cost of more than £45,000) by a huge Great Hall, porte-cochère and reception rooms, to designs of Dobson's son-in-law Sidney Smirke. The hall, a towering room, was modelled on the chapel of Hampton Court Palace. Vast new service wings were also added.

By the 1920's this had become unmanageable, and in 1932 Dobson and Smirke's additions, the service ranges, and the link between Bonomi's 'chapel-like' range and the tower, were demolished by the 4th Earl of Durham. The remaining part was occupied for some time, but after the 1939-45 war Lord Durham made over the estate to his son, Viscount Lambton, who chose to live in the smaller, early 18th century Biddick Hall on the estate. Lambton Castle was leased to Durham County Council in 1966 for teacher training accommodation, but is now disused. Amazingly, two eighteenth century rooms from Harraton Hall survived the successive rebuildings and still exist. On the south side, some of Ignatius Bonomi's 1820's rooms, with Tudor details, survive.

South-west view (J. Jamieson, Durham at the opening of the twentieth century, 1906)

Entrance front, showing Smirke's Great Hall (Newcastle Central Library)

THE DEANERY, Chester-le-Street

Until the Reformation Chester was a collegiate church with a Dean. In 1606 James I granted the Deanery estate, east of the church, to the Hedworths. It was a plain, rendered house with a high roof pierced by dormers. John Hedworth died 1747 and was succeeded by two daughters; one married John Hylton of Hylton Castle (q.v.), the other Sir Ralph Milbanke of Seaham, and Halnaby, Yorkshire. In 1857 their descendants Charles Joliffe and Lady Byron were owners. The Deanery was tenanted, in the early 19th century by John Morton Davidson, who improved the house and grounds, and in 1834 by Edward Johnson of Newcastle.

The Deanery, seen from across the Wear by W. Beilby (The Duke of Northumberland)

WHITEHILL HALL, Chester-le-Street

Whitehill, to the west of Chester, was the Millot family seat from the 1400's until John Millot died 1747. A keen huntsman and gambler, he was shown on a screen long preserved at Whitehill. In the early 19th century the owner John Cookson remodelled Whitehill in a style typical of c.1830. The old centre was fronted by a colonnade and flanked by wings with shallow bay-windows. There was blank panelling between the storeys; all was under a low-pitched roof with deeply overhanging eaves. The architect is unknown. In 1858 Mrs. Cookson was the owner, in 1894 Charles Rollo Barrett. It was demolished in recent years for housing.

Whitehill Hall (J. Jamieson, Durham at the opening of the twentieth century, 1906)

COCKEN HALL, near Chester-le-Street

A little-known house in a fine setting beside the River Wear. Writers praised the picturesque beauties of cliffs, hanging oak woods, terrace-walks, and views of Finchale Abbey ruins. An 18th century engraving shows a 17th century house with wings, and straight avenues and vistas (altered and softened later in the century).

At the Dissolution the Finchale Abbey lands passed to John and Isabel Hilton of Newcastle. Isabel's first husband was Ralph Carr, and Carr descendants owned Cocken until the early 19th century.

Richard Warner, visiting Cocken in 1802, found that "the small but select collection of pictures which rendered Cocken Hall one of the shew places of Durham" had been removed, the oak woods were felled, "the walks neglected, and all the elegancies of the place destroyed." In 1804 Teresian sisters, expelled from Lier in Belgium, moved to Cocken from the Carrs' house at St. Helen Auckland. They stayed until 1830, when a coal mine was opened nearby, then went to Field House, near Darlington. In 1834 Cocken was occupied by "Mr. Crawford, a viewer".

William Standish Carr (1807-1856) of Cocken succeeded his kinsman Frank Hall Standish of Duxbury Park, Lancashire, in 1840, changed his name to Standish, and in 1844 altered Cocken (*Durham Chronicle*, 25 Oct. 1844). Photographs show the house halved in size, with most old features obliterated. Cocken was later the seat of John Gully (1783-1863), prize fighter, racehorse owner and coal-owner, and in 1906 of Ralph Milbanke Hudson.

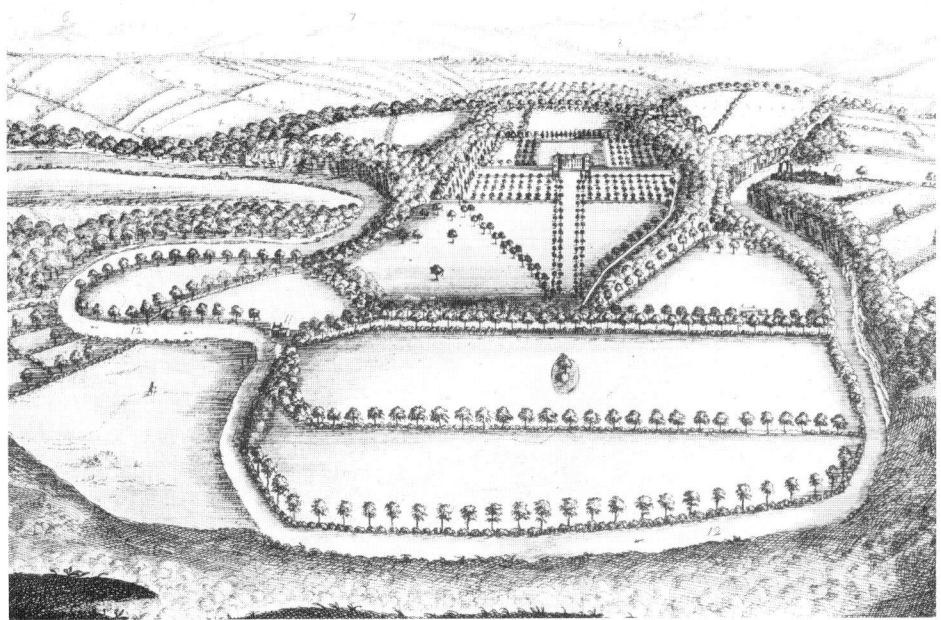

Cocken Hall, part of 18th century engraving (British Library, K. Top. XII, 38)

Cocken Hall (Durham County Record Office)

NEWTON HALL, Durham

A handsome house north of Durham, Newton Hall was built c.1730 for Sir Henry Liddell, later Lord Ravensworth (d.1784). It was brick with stone dressings, and an applied portico of fluted Ionic pilasters supporting a frieze and cornice. In 1812 Sir Thomas Liddell sold Newton Hall to William Russell of Brancepeth, and in 1834 it was the residence of Henry Spearman, recorder of Durham. In the late 19th century it became a County Lunatic Asylum, and was a barracks in the 1914-18 War. Afterwards it was empty and fell into disrepair and was demolished in 1926. A housing estate now covers the site.

Newton Hall (Durham University Library, Edis collection)

HOUGHAM HALL, near Durham

A moated stone manor house of the 16th century, and latterly a farm, Houghall was demolished in 1966. It was part of the lands of the Dean and Chapter of Durham, and became part of the endowment of the University of Durham in the 1830's. The front was a typical farmhouse, but at the back was a taller 17th century wing with mullioned and transomed windows under square hood-moulds. Inside was a Jacobean well staircase with bold balusters, a fine Tudor arched fireplace, and a secret chamber in the main chimney.

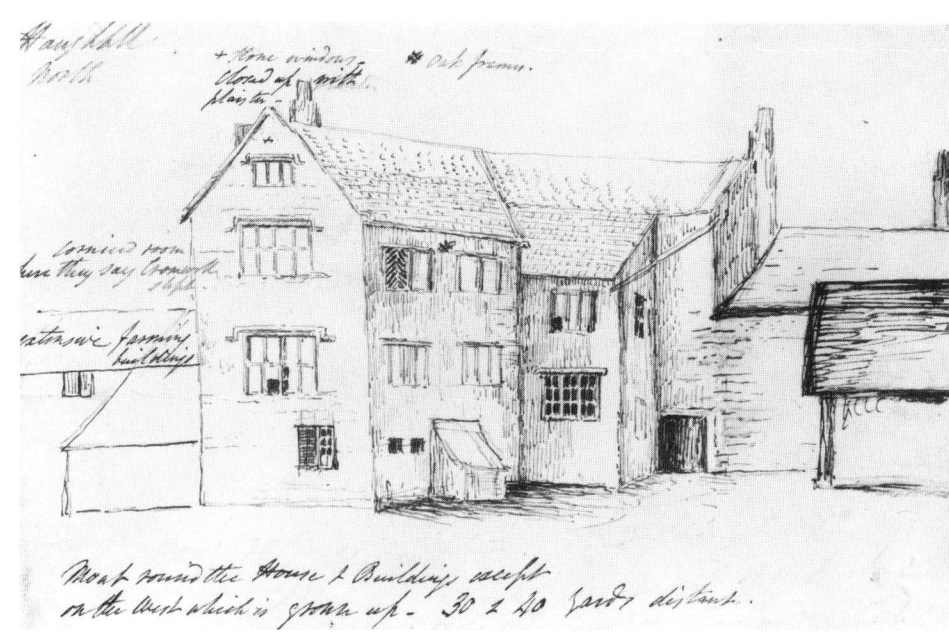

Houghall Hall (Durham University Library, Surtees Raine MS.V.15, fol.40)

HETTON HALL, Hetton-le-Hole

Hetton Hall stood to the west of the town, in a low position near Hetton Burn. The estate was bought in 1686 by John Spearman. His grandson John Spearman (d.1746) sold Hetton to the Countess of Strathmore, who gave it to her younger son Thomas Lyon (1741-96). By 1834 Hetton was called 'an excellent deserted manor house', and by 1857 it was the seat of Nicholas Wood (d.1865), mining engineer. The Hall's mid-19th century style suggests that Wood rebuilt it. By 1902 it was described as 'unoccupied', and after falling into disrepair, was demolished in 1923.

Hetton Hall shortly before demolition (Beamish Museum)

DENEHOLME, Horden

Little is known of this strange, half-octagonal house with castellated trimmings.

TRIMDON HALL, near Sedgefield

17th century, with later additions (the front inscribed 'Brian Roper. Anno Dom. 1718'), Trimdon Hall was demolished in the 1960's. In 1856 it was the seat of Anthony Brydon; in 1894 of Dr. William Smith.

Deneholme

COXHOE HALL

High on a south-facing hillside, Coxhoe was a plain classical house of c.1725 given a Gothic trim some years later. It was a seat of John Burdon, who created the landscape gardens at Hardwick Hall, Sedgefield.

The medieval house at Coxhoe belonged to the Blakistons from about 1400 to 1600. Soon afterwards Mary Blakiston married Sir William Kennett of Sellenge, Kent. The Kennetts owned Coxhoe until Mary Kennett married William, 5th Earl of Seaforth, in 1714. Lord Seaforth, a Jacobite, fled abroad after the Old Pretender's failed uprising in 1715, and in 1725 Coxhoe was sold to John Burdon. Burdon was from South Shields, and was the youngest of 18 children.

Burdon rebuilt the Hall soon afterwards. It is not clear when the Gothic features — battlements and a few pointed windows — were added. Burdon bought Hardwick in 1748 and set about its landscaping, employing James Paine to design his garden buildings and John Bell, a Durham builder, to execute them. The expense bankrupted him, and in 1758 he sold Coxhoe to John Swinburn, husband of his niece Sarah Burdon.

Inside was some good plasterwork, perhaps designed by Paine and executed by Giuseppe Cortese (who worked at Hardwick and at nearby Elemore Hall). The entrance hall opened into the stairhall through a doorway of Venetian shape. The stairhall had plaster panels, swags and cartouches; and in the drawing room was rococo work. There was an exuberant chimneypiece, with crossed palms and a bracket above, and a swirling ceiling with a female figure in the centre. Unfortunately the only known photograph does not show the ceiling completely.

Coxhoe Hall (J. Jamieson, Durham at the opening of the 20th century, 1906

Entrance hall (Durham University Library, Edis collection)

William Swinburn succeeded his brother John in 1774, and from him it passed to Major William Swinburn; but difficulties about the inheritance led to a Chancery order to sell Coxhoe in 1794. There were several short ownerships and tenancies, including that of Edward Moulton Barrett and his wife in the early 1800's. Their daughter the poet Elizabeth Barrett (Browning) was born at Coxhoe in 1806. In 1817 Anthony Wilkinson of Durham bought the Hall, and in 1850 it passed to Thomas Wood, a mining engineer. He made several alterations and additions, including a single-storey billiard room which continued the castellated style. He later moved to Surrey but was succeeded at Coxhoe by his son, William Henry Wood, a coal owner, who lived there until his death in 1910. His wife continued at Coxhoe until 1928, and his son succeeded her.

Coxhoe was offered for sale in 1938, and was bought by the East Hetton Colliery Company. There had been pits nearby since the early 19th century. It was requisitioned in the 1939-45 war, and used to house Italian and German prisoners. Afterwards it was occupied by squatters, vandalised, and condemned by the National Coal Board, which claimed that coal workings beneath it had made it unsafe. It was demolished by 1956.

In the time of the Woods the hillside was said to be inhabited by innumerable tame rabbits of many colours and varieties, now all gone.

Detail of plasterwork above staircase window (RCHM England)

Drawing room
(Durham University Library, Edis collection)

MAINSFORTH HALL, near Sedgefield

Mainsforth was a seat of the Surtees family, and was chiefly notable as the home of the Durham historian Robert Surtees (1779-1834), whose four volumes of county history were published in 1816-40 (the fourth edited by his friend James Raine). The work, still incomplete, was continued by Surtees' relation Sir Herbert Conyers Surtees (1858-1933).

In 1708 the Huttons sold the Mainsforth estate to Robert Surtees of Ryton and Edward Surtees of Crawbrook, and Mainsforth Hall was rebuilt by the Surtees about 1725. It was a modest house, five bays, two-and-a-half storeys, with quoined corners, moulded window surrounds and a high, plain parapet. It was cement rendered. At least one of the rooms had oak panelling. Fordyce (1857) described it as 'a good specimen of those peculiarly English mansions in which comfort and elegance are happily united.'

After the death of Robert Surtees, his library, manuscripts and pictures were sold to clear debts. Many of the pictures had been drawn by Surtees' father. His widow Anne (1785-1868) continued to live at Mainsforth until her death. She was succeeded by Charles Freville Surtees (1823-1906), of the Redworth Hall branch of the family, and he was succeeded by Sir Herbert Conyers Surtees.

Mainsforth was eventually close to the large industrial village of Ferryhill. After the 1939-45 war it fell into disrepair. It was reported empty in 1952, and was demolished in 1962. A modern house now stands on the site; the old gatepiers, rusticated and with pineapple finials, survive.

Mainsforth Hall (J. Davidson)

Mainsforth 1944 (RCHM England)

Mainsforth Hall, street front, 1962 (Evening Despatch, 13 June 1962)

Oak parlour (H. C. Surtees and H. R. Leighton, Records of the family of Surtees, 1925)

THRISLINGTON HALL, near Ferryhill

A mid-17th century house, once of some distinction, with sash-windows, rusticated door surrounds and double gables. Inside was a good staircase and a ceiling with roses and fleur-de-lys. It had a chequered history. In the 18th century it belonged to Sir Thomas Robinson of Rokeby, Yorkshire, who sold it to Hendry Hopper of Durham. In 1794 it was 'going to ruin', but was evidently repaired later. By 1834 it had passed to Hopper's nephew Robert Hopper Williamson; in 1856 it was owned by the Revd. Robert Williamson and occupied by Joseph Atkinson; and in 1894 by William Morson. By the 1970's, when Thrislington Quarry encroached, it had lost a central bay of windows; by 1976 it was ruinous; it was offered to Sedgefield Council, but in 1979 it was condemned as irreparable and demolished.

Thrislington Hall (Evening Despatch, 4 April 1975)

HAWTHORN TOWER.
Easington

Although Hawthorn Tower had a medieval look, it was entirely 19th century. The architect John Dobson of Newcastle built it in 1821 for Major Anderson, and it was enlarged c.1850 by Thomas Moore of Sunderland. It was a convincing composition of towers, gables, Gothic windows and an oriel, originally rendered, though this covering gradually crumbled away to reveal a curious 'crazy' stonework effect.

Hawthorn Dene, a deep, narrow ravine running down to the sea between Easington and Seaham, belonged in the 18th century to Milbankes of Seaham and Halnaby, Yorkshire. At the mouth of the Dene, overlooking the rocky coast, Admiral Milbanke (d.1805) built a summer house, Sailor's Hall, in the late 18th century. By 1816 it was in ruins, but it must have been partly repaired, since in 1865 it belonged to Mark Snowdon.

Major Anderson built his Gothic mansion close by. It was originally called Hawthorn Hive Cottage. In 1856 it belonged to his representatives, and later it belonged to the Pembertons of Low Barnes, Sunderland. Richard Pemberton (b.1831) was the owner in 1897. It was occupied until the 1939-45 war, but soon afterwards was abandoned and became ruinous.

Hawthorn Tower (J. Davidson)

Hawthorn Tower, front (Durham City Library)

Hawthorn Tower (The Northern Echo)

WOLVISTON HALL, near Stockton

Wolviston's early history is obscure. It had sash windows, a small portico, and battlements. It could have been Rose Villa, seat of Robert Appleby, described as "a neat modern mansion" in 1834. In 1857 Fordyce noted "its beautiful lawn, greenhouse, and vineries". It passed from Thomas Appleby to Thomas Skinner, and was occupied by Augustus Friedrichsen and Wright Clunie.

From the 1880's Wolviston was occupied by the Websters, who had bought it from Captain Young. At the rear was a huge range of glasshouses flanking box-edged parterres. After the death of Captain Webster and his wife, their son Rowland moved to his other house at Unthank, Haltwhistle, Northumberland, in 1942. In 1943 the Hall housed German and Italian prisoners of war.

After the war the Hall was converted into flats. Mrs. Linton bought it and lived in the largest flat. After her death builders bought the Hall, demolished it and in 1966 built Manor Court.

Wolviston Hall (J. Jamieson, Durham at the opening of the 20th Century, 1906)

BLAKISTON HALL, Norton

A 17th century brick building, seven-bay, two storey, held by the Blakiston family for 300 years until Sir Thomas Blakiston sold it to Alexander Davison, Newcastle merchant. Thomas Davison Bland (b.1745) inherited Kippax Park, Yorkshire. Blakiston was sold c.1800 to William Russell of Brancepeth. Hutchinson (1794) called it "a spacious old edifice, but lately pulled down." A small part remained, and in 1856 was occupied by Joseph Wanless a market gardener.

Wolviston Hall, front (P. Menzies)

TUNSTALL MANOR,
West Hartlepool

The area round the Ward Jackson Park in West Hartlepool was developed in the second half of the nineteenth century to accommodate the wealthier residents of what had become one of England's largest ports. Ralph Ward Jackson, the founder of this fledgling new town fell from grace amid scandal but his mantle was taken up by the likes of Sir William Gray, the fabulously rich shipbuilder.

Sir William commissioned the building, as late as 1898, of Tunstall Manor, the town's grandest and most bizarre house. His architect was T. Lewis Banks, who had designed the adjoining Tunstall Court in 1894.

Externally it was a mish-mash of styles. A large port-cochère was glued to the building by two Scottish baronial turrets flanking a high gable with a distinctly continental flavour. The remainder of the building was loosely in the Elizabethan style.

The real shock was hiding inside —a two-storey galleried Moorish hall with arcades straight from the Alhambra. It was lit by day from a central lantern and by night from Moorish electric candelabra, enriched by numerous incense burners. The atmosphere must have been heady indeed. Those on the gallery wishing to sample it could peep through oriel windows in lattice work on to the Moorish furniture below.

The dining room was a more conventional nineteenth century Tudor, with an orgy of carving.

Tunstall Manor (Hartlepool Museums Service)

The Moorish Hall (Hartlepool Museums Service)

In spite of all this, or perhaps because of it, Tunstall Manor lasted for a mere 28 years and was replaced in 1926 by a more modest house in stockbroker Tudor.

Tunstall Manor during demolition (Hartlepool Museums Service)

GREATHAM HALL, Hartlepool

When Dormer Parkhurst became Master of the Greatham Hospital in 1711 he found the buildings in a ruinous condition. In 1725 he rebuilt Greatham Hall. In 1820 the garden front was stuccoed and in 1857 it was extended.

Its most celebrated resident was Ralph Ward Jackson, the founder of West Hartlepool, who rented part of it in the mid 19th century.

During the Second World War the cellars were used as air raid shelters but the building could not withstand the bulldozers which moved in in 1962. There is a modern house on the site incorporating a small part of the original.

Greatham Hall (A. Harrison)

LONG NEWTON HALL, near Stockton

Long Newton was purchased in 1635 by Sir Henry Vane of Raby Castle, and settled on his second son Sir George Vane (d.1679) in 1640. Sir Henry Vane succeeded to the estate in 1793, married Frances, daughter of John Tempest of Wynyard Park, and united the Wynyard and Long Newton estates. He lived at Wynyard and kept racehourses at Long Newton. His granddaughter Frances Anne Vane-Tempest married the 3rd Marquess of Londonderry. Their interests lay in rebuilding Wynyard Park in the 1820's. Long Newton Hall, a large brick house sketched on an estate survey (1752), and described by Hutchinson (1794) as "modern and handsome", was demolished before 1823.

WOODSIDE HALL, Eaglescliffe

The history of Woodside Hall, a large Victorian mansion now mostly demolished and replaced by a school, has not been established.

BILLINGHAM HALL

A short-lived Victorian villa of unremarkable appearance, built north of the village near the station in the 1870's. There was a succession of owners: in 1881 James Graves, shipowner, broker and Hartlepool alderman; in 1894 C. J. Watson; Captain Jesse Lilly bought it in 1897, and the Nielson family in 1909. In the 1920's, J. McGovern, of Furness Shipbuilding, lived in it; and in 1935 it was demolished for a housing estate, part of the great expansion of Billingham to house north Teesside chemical and other industrial workers.

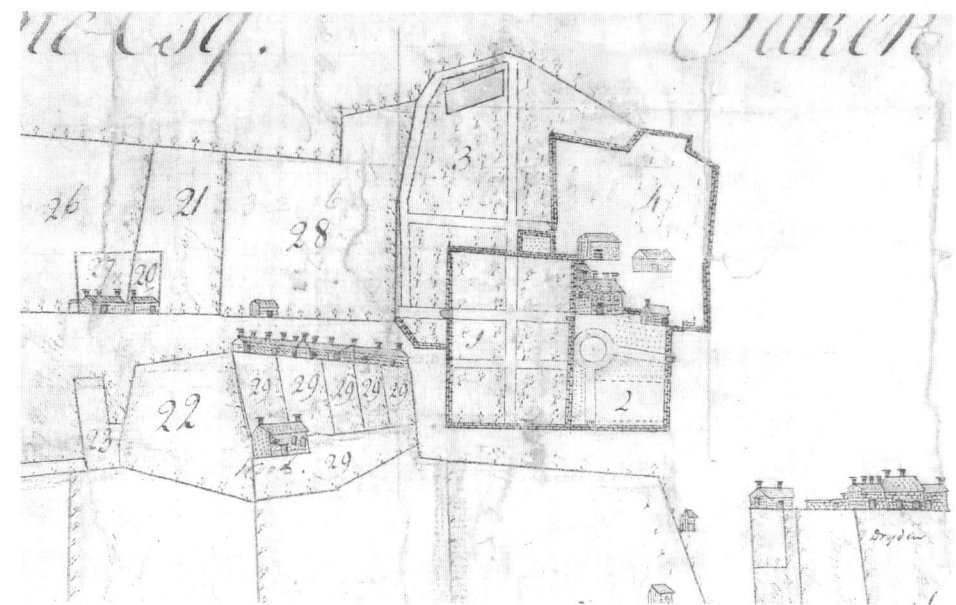

Detail from 'A plan of the Mannor of Longnewton belonging to Lyonell Vane', by Toby Ward, 1752 (Durham County Record Office, Londonderry Papers)

Woodside Hall (P. Menzies)

ELTON HALL, near Stockton

Elton Hall was demolished c.1910 and replaced with the present elegant Edwardian mansion. In the 18th century the Shaftos of Whitworth owned the estate. Later George Sutton (1735-1817) owned Elton House and enlarged it, creating fine landscaped grounds. His great-nephew George William Sutton (1781-1853) made alterations and extensions in 1829; other alteraions were made by his nephew Lieutenant-Colonel Sleigh, who built a large greenhouse. A view of the Hall shows an 18th century facade with a pedimented porch, a Venetian window at the side, and the elegant conservatory. Sutton's second son John Stapylton Sutton (1832-1917) sold Elton Hall c.1900 to Thomas Appleby (d.1909), who rebuilt the Hall. Appleby's son Stanley Appleby sold Elton in 1925 to Robert Ropner, second son of Sir Robert Ropner, shipbuilder.

Elton Hall (John Brewster, Stockton-upon-Tees, 2nd ed., 1829)

BISHOP'S MANOR HOUSE, Darlington

The Bishop's Manor House stood near the church and the River skerne, where the Civic Centre is now. It became ruinous in the 17th century, but was restored by Bishop Cosin. It was neglected in the 18th century, and was sub-let by the life-tenant, the Bishop's housekeeper, to the town as a poor-house. In 1806 Darlington bought it outright, and built an additional building of a pedimented centre and two wings. In 1834 the old building was said to retain 'many traces of antiquity in its low arches, thick walls and long passages'. It was a long building with windows of all periods from mediæval to 18th century. On the street front were three lancets, indicating perhaps a former chapel.

Bishop's Manor House, late 18th century (Darlington Centre for Local Studies)

BLACKWELL HILL, Darlington

Situated on the banks of the Tees near Blackwell Hall, Blackwell Hill was a conventional Gothic villa, of red brick with stone dressings, designed c.1870 by G. G. Hoskins of Darlington for Eliza Barclay, widow of Robert Barclay, and sister of John Church Backhouse. It was later the home of Edward (1840-1911) and Rachel Backhouse Maunsey, later of G. M. Harroway, and finally John Neasham. It was demolished c.1972 for Farr Holme houses.

Blackwell Hill (Darlington Centre for Local Studies)

BRANKSOME HALL, Darlington

To the north-west of Darlington, Branksome Hall was a conventional Victorian villa, originally called Westfield and built for Robert Teesdale. It was bought in 1852 by John Kitching, a railway engineer and director, and doubled in size by the addition of a large wing in 17th century style, with a rather wide central bay window of two storeys and dormers capped with triangular and segmental pediments. The name Branksome was inspired by a poem by Sir Walter Scott. Kitching had a notable collection of furniture, paintings, porcelain and statuary. He died in 1935 and his seven surviving bachelor sons lived at Branksome until 1955. In that year they sold the estate of 230 acres to Darlington Council. The estate was developed for housing for the disabled and elderly, and the Hall was demolished in 1978 for housing.

Branksome Hall (Evening Despatch, April 1953)

WOODBURN, Darlington

On the road to Coniscliffe, Woodburn was built c.1870 by John Pease for his daughter Sophia. For her sister Mary Anna he built the adjoining and similar Elm Ridge, which survives. Woodburn was a huge Victorian Gothic house of stone, with many gables, turrets and tall chimneys, by G. G. Hoskins. Sophia Pease married Sir Theodore Fry (d.1912), businessman, philanthropist and M.P. for Darlington, 1880. He formed a large collection of Greek and Etruscan pottery. After Lady Fry's death in 1912 he left Woodburn. The house and six acres were bought in 1913 by the Clayhills family. The last occupant was Thomas Clayhills-Henderson (1836-1933), solicitor. Woodburn was demolished in 1935.

Woodburn (Darlington centre for Local Studies)

WOODSIDE, Darlington

Woodside, in a vaguely Italianate style, was built in 1842 for John C. Hopkins. According to the *Durham Chronicle*, 8 July 1842, the architect and builder was Thomas Robson junior.

About 1848 Woodside was bought by John Harris, Quaker civil engineer and railway contractor, with interests in brickmaking, ironworks and the development of Middlesbrough. He added a huge conservatory designed by Richardson and Ross of Darlington, and a tower and wing, in a style similar to the original.

Harris died in 1869, and Woodside became the home of Gurney Pease (1839-72), and his widow, until the early 20th century. It was demolished in the 1930's for housing development; the kitchen garden and vinery survived as a market garden until 1984.

Woodside (Northern Echo)

NEASHAM HALL, near Darlington

In 1970 Sir John Wrightson demolished Neasham Hall and replaced it with a much smaller house on the same site, to designs by Sir Martyn Beckett. The old Hall, in fine grounds running down to the River Tees, was much extended in 1834-7 for Colonel Cookson by John Dobson of Newcastle.

The 18th century Hall was probably the centre, with its two bow windows rising through three storeys, somewhat like Blackwell Hall, Darlington (q.v.). Dobson added two large wings, with a columned entrance porch on the side, and gave the main facade an Elizabethan trim on the parapets and gables.

The Neasham estate was purchased in 1698 from Sir William Blackett by Charles Turner of Kirkleatham, Yorkshire. The Turners held Neasham through the 18th century, but Sir Charles Turner (1773-1810) sold it to William Wrightson. Thomas Wrightson sold Neasham to Colonel Cookson, who commissioned Dobson to extend the Hall. In 1857 it was the seat of James Cookson; by 1896 it belonged to Sir Thomas Wrightson. In 1904 a massive music room was added.

Neasham Hall (Hon. Lady Wrightson)

Neasham Hall (Hon. Lady Wrightson)

Boudoir (Hon. Lady Wrightson)

Dining room (Hon. Lady Wrightson)

Staircase (Hon. Lady Wrightson)

Music room (Hon. Lady Wrightson)

BLACKWELL HALL, Darlington

Blackwell, south of Darlington, belonged to the Allans from the late 16th century. They came from Brockhouse, Staffordshire. Their main house, Blackwell Grange, still stands (now the Europa Hotel). It was the home of James Allan (1712-90) and his son George Allan (1736-1800), collectors of books and manuscripts. George Allan gave his notes on Durham to William Hutchinson, first historian of the county. James Allan's younger son, Robert Allan, succeeded to the unentailed estates, and either he or his son John Allan (d.1844) built Blackwell Hall. It was a brick building, with wings running back from a narrow front. This front had two-storey bows, classical below, rising to Gothic castellated turrets. Inside was a cantilever staircase and two Adam-style chimneypieces.

John Allan was succeeded by his nephew Robert Henry Allan (d.1879), while William (Robert's brother) had Blackwell Grange. The heir to both was a cousin, Sir Henry Havelock-Allan (1830-97), soldier. His son Sir Henry Havelock-Allan sold Blackwell in 1930 to W. Stanley Robinson, Darlington auctioneer. He lived in the Hall for 10 years, and to prevent "houses of the bungalow type", built some large houses in the grounds. In 1940 Alexander Dickson, managing director of the Estate Company, made the Hall a private residential hotel. It continued, with a few residents and regular visitors, until the mid-1960's. It was sold in 1963 to Raine Brothers, building contractors. Houses were built in the grounds and the Hall was to become six flats. By 1965, however, reports of deteriorating brickwork and "worm infestation" led to the Hall's demolition.

Blackwell Hall, rear view (Durham County Council)

Blackwell Hall, front (Durham County Council)

RED HALL,
Haughton-le-Skerne, Darlington

Philip Wyatt (d.1835), "brilliant but feckless" youngest son of James Wyatt, architect, designed few buildings. He quarrelled with patrons, was inefficient, and in 1833 was imprisoned for debt. Several of his buildings were proficient essays in various styles: Conishead Priory, Lancashire, 1821-36, was Perpendicular Gothic; Wynyard Park, County Durham, 1822-30, was monumentally neoclassical. Red Hall, designed for Captain Robert Colling "on the spot and on the spur of the moment" in 1830, was Tudor Gothic.

Red Hall stood on the Skerne, opposite the village. There was an older, red-brick house (the colour probably providing the name; there were also "Blue Hall" and "White Hall" in the village). Robert Colling of Long Newton bought the house in 1697, and his family held it for two centuries. Wyatt replaced the brick house with a stone building, tall and with many gables. Its height was somewhat exaggerated by the attenuation of many of the elevations and oriel windows.

In the 1920's the Hall was bought by the Haggie family. In the late 1950's and early 1960's several proposals were made to use the estate for housing or light industry. In 1965 Darlington Council bought the estate for £35,000. Housing was planned, and a riding-school was licensed to use the Hall and grounds. In 1967 "Darlington's first factory-made houses" were erected here. Development was inexorable, yet Red Hall stood, empty and increasingly dilapidated, until 1984.

Red Hall (Evening Despatch, 29 July 1965)

Red Hall (Risbey's Photographers, Darlington)

COCKERTON HALL, Darlington

Cockerton Hall, west of Darlington, was a medieval house probably owned by the Nevilles, Earls of Westmorland. The garden front retained several Gothic windows, indicating medieval work.

In 1745 Cockerton passed to William Wrightson (1714-1806), a relation of the Neasham Wrightsons (q.v.). His daughter Nanny (1750-1829) was extremely wealthy, apparently remodelled the Hall front in 1825, and left Cockerton to her nephew Richard Wrightson (d.1830). Wrightson found £8000 in coins and banknotes in the Hall, and made his servant carry it in a butter-basket to Backhouse's Bank in Darlington, while he followed with a shotgun. He left his estates to his widow Eliza, by a will written on a half-sheet of notepaper. His sister, who would otherwise have succeeded, later claimed that the will was a forgery, and the celebrated 'Cockerton will case', which caused much local excitement, was contested to the House of Lords in 1844-50, being finally decided in Eliza's favour.

Eliza married Thomas Topham (d.1873). He left Cockerton to his brother, the Revd. John Topham. The Hall was let to tenants. Mrs. Dodshun ran it as a ladies' school, 1841-61, and after her, Miss Riddel. Later the Hall was occupied by Alfred Jobson, colliery agent for the Peases, and by the Stocks, Jeffreys and Cradock families. In 1920 Charles Freeman Thomas, formerly of Hurworth Manor, bought it, and lived there until 1946. In 1946 a cinema chain bought the Hall and leased it to Darlington Youth Club. In the 1950's, the Post Office used it for storage. It was demolished in 1964.

Cockerton Hall, front (Darlington Centre for Local Studies)

Garden front (Darlington Centre for Local Studies)

BIBLIOGRAPHY

William Bourn, *History of the Parish of Ryton*, 1896.
William Bourn, *Whickham Parish: its history, antiquities and industries*, 1893.
Herbert Conyers-Surtees, *The history of St. Helen Auckland and West Auckland*, 1924 (and other parishes, completing Surtees' history).
Country Life magazine:
  H. Avray Tipping, 'Streatlam Castle, Durham, a seat of the Earl of Strathmore', 18 December 1915.
  Christopher Hussey, 'Gibside, County Durham, a property of the Earl of Strathmore', 8-15 February 1952.
  Christopher Hussey, 'Lambton Castle, Durham, the property of Viscount Lambton', 24-31 March 1966.
  Peter Meadows, 'Palatinate patronage', 14 December 1989.
A description of Bishop Auckland, including the Castle and Park, and several gentlemen's seats in the neighbourhood, 1820.
James J. Dodd, *History of the Urban District of Spennymoor*, 1897.
Tom Faulkner and Andrew Greg, *John Dobson, Newcastle architect 1787-1865*, 1987.
William Fordyce, *The history and antiquities of the County Palatine of Durham*, 1857.
Joan M. Hewitt, *The township of Heworth*, 1990.
George B. Hodgson, *The history of South Shields*, 1924.
William Hutchinson, *The history and antiquities of the County Palatine of Durham*, 1785-94.
J. Jamieson, *Durham at the opening of the twentieth century: contemporary biographies*, ed. T. Pike, 1906.
Henry Leighton, *Memorials of old Durham*, 1910.
Adrian Liddell, *An illustrated history of Wolviston village*, 1988.
James Macaulay, *The Gothic Revival 1745-1845*, 1975.
E. Mackenzie and M. Ross, *An historical, topographical and descriptive view of the County Palatine of Durham*, 1834.
F. W. D. Manders, *History of Gateshead*, 1973.
G. E. Milburn and S. T. Miller, *Sunderland – River Town and People*, 1988.
George Neasham, *Views of mansions in the Lanchester and Derwent valleys*, 1884.
Nikolaus Pevsner and Elizabeth Williamson, *The buildings of England: County Durham*, 2nd ed., 1983.
Proceedings of the Society of Antiquaries of Newcastle: 3rd series II, no. 17 (1906), 'Old Park, Co. Durham.'
  4th series III, no. 23 (1928), 'Hilton Castle, County Durham'.
Douglas W. Smith, *Herrington and its folk*, 1987.
Robert Surtees, *The history and antiquities of the County Palatine of Durham*, 1816-40.
Henry Thorold, *County Durham, A Shell guide*, 1980.
Robin Walton, *History of Coxhoe*, 1986.
Richard Warner, *A tour through the northern counties of England and the borders of Scotland*, 1802.
W. Whellan and Co., *History, topography and directory of the County Palatine of Durham*, 1856 (2nd ed., 1894).
Neville Whittaker, *The old halls and manor houses of County Durham*, 1975.
Winlaton and District Local History Society, *A history of Blaydon*, 1975.

ACKNOWLEDGEMENTS

A book such as this makes much use of the knowledge of local historians and enthusiasts, through published work and personal contact. For help on specific points we are indebted to Beverley Bagnall, Eileen Carnaffin, Lillian Dixon, Lord Eden of Winton, Nick Lufts, Paul Menzies, Roger Norris, Martin Roberts, Peter Ryder and Neville Whittaker. Special thanks are due to Jim Davidson for his hospitality and kindness in sharing his huge collection of country house postcards; and to Lucinda Lambton, for willingly writing the foreword.

For permission to reproduce photographs we are grateful to: Beamish, the North of England Open Air Museum, County Durham; The Bowes Museum, Barnard Castle; The British Library; *Country Life*; Darlington Centre for Local Studies; Durham County Council, Arts, Libraries and Museums Department, County Record Office, Environment Department; Durham Dean and Chapter Library; Durham University Library; Gateshead Library; Hartlepool Museum Service; Mrs. E. Kennewell; The Marquess of Londonderry; Newcastle upon Tyne City Libraries and Arts; The University of Newcastle upon Tyne; *The Northern Echo*, Darlington; His Grace the Duke of Northumberland; Northumberland County Record Office; RIBA/British Architectural Library; The Royal Commission on the Historical Monuments of England; South Tyneside Borough Council; *The Sunderland Echo*; Tyne & Wear Museums Service and The Hon. Lady Wrightson.

Peter Meadows
Cambridge University Library

Edward Waterson
Carter Jonas, York

November 1993

INDEX

Name	Page
ASHBROOKE HALL, Sunderland	46
BILLINGHAM HALL	62
BINCHESTER HALL, Bishop Auckland	10
BIRTLEY HALL	29
BISHOP'S MANOR HOUSE, Darlington	63
BLACKWELL HALL, Darlington	68
BLACKWELL HILL, Darlington	64
BRADLEY HALL, Wolsingham	23
BRANKSOME HALL, Darlington	64
BROADWOOD HALL, Lanchester	15
CLEADON COTTAGE, near South Shields	37
COCKEN HALL, near Chester-le-Street	51
COCKERTON HALL, Darlington	70
CONSETT HALL	23
COXHOE HALL	54
CROOK HALL, Consett	13
DEANERY, Chester-le-Street	50
DECKHAM'S HALL, Gateshead	31
DENEHOLME, Horden	53
ELTON HALL, near Stockton	63
ELVASTON HALL, Ryton	28
ESHWOOD HALL, New Brancepeth	15
FARNACRES, Gateshead	29
FORD HALL, Sunderland	44
GATESHEAD PARK HOUSE	30
GIBSIDE	20
GREATHAM HALL, near West Hartlepool	61
GREENCROFT HALL, Lanchester	14
HARRATON HALL, Chester-le-Street	47
HAWTHORN TOWER, Easington	58
HELMINGTON HALL, Willington	11
HERRINGTON HALL, Sunderland	41
HETTON HALL, Hetton-le-Hole	53
HEWORTH WHITE HOUSE	35
HOPPYLAND PARK, Bedburn	9
HOUGHALL HALL, Durham	52
HYLTON CASTLE, Sunderland	42
LAMBTON CASTLE, Chester-le-Street	48
LITTLE USWORTH HALL, Washington	39
LONG NEWTON HALL, near Stockton	62
LOW BARNES, Sunderland	45
MAINSFORTH HALL, near Sedgefield	56
NEASHAM HALL, near Darlington	66
NEWTON HALL, Durham	52
NEWTON CAP HALL, Bishop Auckland	10
NORTH BIDDICK HALL, Washington	40
OLD PARK, Spennymoor	12
PALLION, Sunderland	45
PARK HEAD HALL, Winlaton	28
RAVENSWORTH CASTLE, near Gateshead	16
RED HALL, Haughton-le-Skerne	69
REDHEUGH HALL, Gateshead	32
RYTON HOUSE	24
SALTWELL HALL, Gateshead	34
SALTWELL TOWERS, Gateshead	34
SHERIFF HILL HALL, Gateshead	33
SIMONSIDE HALL, South Shields	37
SNOTTERTON HALL, Staindrop	8
STANLEY HALL, near Tanfield	13
STELLA HALL, Blaydon	26
STREATLAM CASTLE, near Barnard Castle	6
THOMPSON'S HALL, South Shields	36
THORNHILL HOUSE, Sunderland	41
THRISLINGTON HALL, near Ferryhill	57
TUNSTALL MANOR, West Hartlepool	60
USWORTH HOUSE, Washington	39
WESTOE HALL, South Shields	36
WHITBURN HALL	38
WHITEHILL HALL, Chester-le-Street	50
WHITWORTH HALL, Spennymoor	11
WINLATON HALL	25
WOLVISTON HALL, near Stockton	59
WOODBURN, Darlington	65
WOODSIDE, Darlington	65
WOODSIDE HALL, Eaglescliffe	62